WHEN DID

White Trash

BECOME THE
NEW NORMAL?

WHEN DID
White Trash
BECOME THE
NEW NORMAL?

A Southern Lady Asks the Impertinent Question

Charlotte Hays

Since 1947
REGNERY
Publishing, Inc.
An Eagle Publishing Company • Washington, DC

Cataloging-in-Publication data on file with the Library of Congress

ISBN 978-1-62157-160-5

Published in the United States by
Regnery Publishing, Inc.
One Massachusetts Avenue NW
Washington, DC 20001
www.Regnery.com

Manufactured in the United States of America

10 9 8 7 6 5 4 3 2 1

Books are available in quantity for promotional or premium use. Write to Director of Special Sales, Regnery Publishing, Inc., One Massachusetts Avenue NW, Washington, DC 20001, for information on discounts and terms, or call (202) 216-0600.

Distributed to the trade by
Perseus Distribution
250 West 57th Street
New York, NY 10107

For my great-nieces Jenna, Julia, and Sarah—hint, hint

Contents

White Trash Recipes –

for When You Want to Eat (and Drink) Like

Hit Don't Make No Difference

"It is the manners and spirit of a people which preserve a republic in vigour. A degeneracy in these is a canker which soon eats to the heart of its laws and constitution."

—THOMAS JEFFERSON

"I wish I had an extra finger. Then I could grab more cheese balls."

—HONEY BOO BOO
(on learning that her niece was born with three thumbs)

Chapter One

Why Obesity, Tattoos, and Velveeta® Cheese Prove That Arnold Toynbee Was Right

BBC program recently quoted a tattoo "artist," as they are now styled, to the effect that tattooing "used to be the preserve of people who were too lazy to work and too scared to steal."

Now, alas, it is the preserve of one's friends and relatives. I got my first taste of this at a lovely garden party in Richmond, Virginia. I was stopped in my tracks by a recently quite attractive young cousin who now sported a bandana at a rakish angle and a garish jungle on each arm. I didn't know whether to think Jean Lafitte the pirate or maximum security. What would Mama have thought if she'd lived to see White Trash cousins—in hallowed Richmond, no less? Meanwhile, a brilliant young woman of my acquaintance, a scholar at a conservative think tank in Washington, D.C., showed up at a fancy benefit dinner in a little black cocktail dress that revealed shoulders and upper arms extensively covered with tattoos. While trying to avert my eyes, I nevertheless observed a motif of threatening birds that were only marginally less sinister than the creatures in the Hitchcock movie about our feathered friends. Further sign of the impending Apocalypse: she is a tattooed Chi Omega, Chi O being the sorority once exclusive to the most ladylike among us. She wears a "bespoke tattoo," which she designed in consultation with an "artist." In my mind, it bespoke volumes. What it mainly said is that White Trash manners have become the new normal.

You no longer have to be White Trash to do White Trash things. Samantha Cameron, for example, wife of the blue-blooded British Prime Minister David Cameron, has a tattoo, too. It's only a small dolphin on her ankle, but can we agree that this is a look Clementine Churchill and Maggie Thatcher would have avoided? A small dolphin is nothing compared to the elegantly named "tramp stamps" (tattoos on the lower back) or "skank stamps" (tattoos on the rib cage) that are the rage among educated young women in the United States. Even the President of the United States now has to worry that his daughters may succumb to the rage for tattoos. He and the First Lady are trying to prevent that—by threatening that they'll get tattoos, too, if Sasha and Malia do.

Tragically, younger people in general no longer regard the tattoo with disgust. The Pew Research Center for People and the Press reports that 36 percent of Gen Nexters—Americans in the eighteen-to-twenty-five age group—have one. Or, as

Trash vs. Quality

Quality: Serving wine with family dinner
Trash: Making meth with your toddler in the house

Quality: Setting the table properly
Trash: Using your knife to settle a family argument

Quality: Reserving physical intimacy for private settings
Trash: Reserving physical intimacy for the subway

Quality: Showing up for work regularly
Trash: Showing up for work when you feel like it . . . because
hit don't matter, especially not when you've got a
great new video game

Quality: Polite conversation on topics of general interest
Trash: Way too much information

Quality: Sitting down to dinner as a family
Trash: Everybody grabs his own bag of pork rinds

Quality: Having a job
Trash: Going on disability because of mild back pain
(so you can spend more time watching reality shows
about people like yourself)

Quality: Buying things you can afford
Trash: Getting another credit card whenever you max out
the last one

Quality: Brooks Brothers
Trash: Larry the Cable Guy as a fashion icon

Quality: Bicycling through Europe
Trash: A week at Disney World® . . . without the kids

Pew puts it, Gen Nexters "are not afraid to express themselves through their appearance and tattoos are the most popular form of self-expression." Perhaps they should be more afraid. Perhaps we all should be more afraid.

One Must Suffer to Be Beautiful

The rib cage has become the "emerging" spot for tattoos, according to an October 4, 2011, report in the *Denver Post*. The tattoo-ee must be prepared to undergo pain to acquire this disfigurement:

> Once largely reserved for ink veterans who could ride out the agony, the rib cage has become prime real estate—for men and women. "It's the hottest place on the body right now," said Ryan Hewell, owner of Big Easy Tattoo and Piercing in Broomfield.
>
> Don't look for little hearts or four-leaf clovers, the kind of tats plastered on biceps. The people inking their long, wide rib cages want murals—cherry blossom trees, dragons, and, instead of single roses, entire bouquets.

Tattoos have penetrated heretofore inviolate precincts. I went to a school, for example, that sent girls home for chewing gum in public. Times change, but even so this excellent and still-beloved private academy for young Southern ladies and gentlemen is not the kind of place you'd expect to see tattoos, right? Wrong. The new English teacher is introduced in an alum magazine photo that reveals a tattoo. The tattoo is visible because the teacher is wearing a patterned, short-sleeved sports shirt. In my day, male faculty members were considered naked without a coat and tie. But I doubt if there were tattoos that needed covering. I don't want to make too much of the tattoo craze, but could it signal that the end is nigh?

Not that tattoos are the only heralds of doom. Next time you see an unshaven celebrity clad in slept-in blue jeans, thumbing his nose at bourgeois convention, don't think "Cool"—think White Trash! Grunge is a white trash variation. Obesity, backwards baseball caps, and vulgar language nonchalantly uttered in the ATM line are further expressions of White Trash Normal. Diabetes, by the way, is the talismanic White Trash disease, though it should be noted that there are guiltless diabetics who have not brought their suffering upon themselves by White Trash choices. Still, why go to the trouble of cooking a meal that will be eaten around a dinner table when there are so many processed offerings now available to satisfy every transient craving? The elastic waistband is the White Trash fashion statement.

Old White Trash
Hillbillies and rednecks

New White Trash
Reality show contestants

Old White Trash
Not enough visits to the dentist

New White Trash
Too many visits to the plastic surgeon

If you want to see White Trash Normal in full flower, go to the nearest airport. Once upon a time men wore suits and ladies donned dark cottons and gloves to fly. Now trousers at half mast and dirty T-shirts are normal traveling attire. When was the last time you saw a man give his seat to a lady on public transportation?

When I was growing up in the Deep South, people in all walks of life put forth tremendous effort not to be regarded as White Trash—in contrast to people today who risk hepatitis to ape the decorative styles of social deviants. The White Trash ethos used to be summed up by the broken-down tractor permanently bivouacked in the front yard—expressing the White Trash view of life, the utter rejection of physical and mental exertion: "Hit don't make no difference."

You didn't have to aspire to joining the country club to not want to be mistaken for White Trash. Not being White Trash had little to do with money. It had everything to do with choice and effort, with wearing presentable attire, getting your children to Sunday school, paying your bills in a timely fashion, and putting matrimony chronologically in front of motherhood—in other words, acknowledging that there were standards and that the hard work required to meet them was worth the trouble. When did it become scandalous for banks to charge overdraft fees, nowadays a matter for congressional concern? When White Trash money management became the norm.

So call me uptight, but I'm all in favor of adopting the customs of the civilized elements of society over those of criminal gangs—known, by the way, for their trademark monochromatic tattoos, now adapted for the middle class wearer—or people doing hard time. (I know, I know, standards of decency are now culturally insensitive.) The family that once upon a time purchased a fake ancestral portrait to bluff its way upwards may initially have been annoying, but eventually they learned to speak proper English, contribute to charities, and in general to behave in a way that did the faux ancestor proud. Society benefited, and the members of the family benefited. If you listen to the accents in old movies, you'll hear something that sounds like an American version of the "received pronunciation" favored by the BBC. You also see hobos with good manners in movies of a certain vintage. Yes, sometimes people were snobs. But that was better for society than universal vulgarity.

> *Remember when...*
> Little girls aspired to be like Audrey Hepburn or Princess Grace— instead of Snooki?

In the 1960s my grandfather was still being catty about the grandmother of a contemporary of mine who in nineteen ought some year or other had hesitated too long over which fork to pick up at dinner. But guess what? The fork-challenged grandmother had since mastered the intricacies of Victorian silverware placement, improved her command of grammar, and educated her sons at Ivy League schools. She had become, in short, a grand lady, a pillar of our community, a supporter of cultural activities—and her transformation was achieved by choice and hard work; it relied upon a sense that polite society's standards mattered. She probably would have been irritated rather than amused by my grandfather's reminiscences, but by then she no doubt kindly looked down on us as only shabby genteel— and, to our credit, we were. Believe you me, being shabby genteel requires a heck of a lot more work than succumbing to White Trash Normal.

While rejecting White Trash manners didn't cost us any money, it did require a refusal to believe *hit don't make no*

> ## *Not Clear on the Concept*
>
> The word gentleman has become a synonym for a male person. If Jack the Ripper were active today, we'd be hearing some ninny on TV droning on about "the gentleman who murders prostitutes."

difference, an implicit acknowledgement that manners and customs are vulgarized at society's peril. It did not require a chest of fine silver, but it did require caring enough to learn how to set the table properly, at least for an everyday meal. (Today I have a friend who regales me with me with stories of fabulous parties she attended in Washington, D.C., in the Kennedy era but whose granddaughters haven't the foggiest how to set a table!) The rejection of White Trash Normal was a rejection of laziness, the opposite of going on government disability insurance when you aren't sick. It was about bettering oneself rather than worsening oneself. It was about—and here's a word that's sneered at today—respectability.

When my grandfather was a very old man, my mother would stand by the old Dodge staring vaguely into space while her father struggled with his cane around to her side of the car to open the door for her. Several neighbors commented on this. Why couldn't Julia Morgan just open the door for herself and spare the old man? People who said that didn't know my mother or my grandfather. He wanted to open the door for her, and she wanted him to do it, mostly for him—but she did feel entitled to certain privileges on the basis of her sex. Stumbling around to her door helped my grandfather uphold the standards at the very core of his being. I grew up in his house, and I can honestly say that I can't recall once having seen him without a tie. When he plowed in his vegetable garden, he fastidiously hung his jacket—always with a pocket square—on the fence by the parsley bed. He regarded being a gentleman as something worth working for, even as an old man, and gentleman was defined in a way that a janitor could be considered a gentleman if he strove to do the right thing.

Old White Trash
Arkansas Ozarks

New White Trash
New Jersey Shore

Old White Trash
Sleeping with the dog

New White Trash
Putting on the dog

One of my favorite examples of the pull of civilized manners is a true story about a friend of my family from our little Mississippi town. He was a war hero but still a bit rough around the edges (do people still use that expression?). When he fell in love with a judge's daughter, he knew he needed to improve himself, so he went every day during his lunch hour to the house of a lady who set the table and tutored him in proper etiquette. It took a certain amount of humility to do this, but it paid off. He married the judge's daughter, and had a happy life—though she, being aristocratic (in Mississippi, judges' families count as aristocrats), ended up quite eccentric.

The children who came to school from way out in the sticks in pressed clothes and minded their language came from families that had made a similar choice. They were poor but not poor White Trash. White Trash was the boy we all knew who cursed teachers, used bad words, and had failed so many grades that he acquired the distinction of being the only boy at E. E. Bass Junior High School who had a draft board problem. He avoided Vietnam but, sadly, died in a knife fight in prison, no doubt wildly tattooed. That was White Trash.

There was often a tug-of-war between genteel standards and White Trash manners. A friend of mine had one grandmother who bought her a white rabbit fur coat in elementary school. The other grandmother believed more in patent leather shoes, thank you notes in ink, and white gloves (yes, this was some time ago). What's wrong with fake mink stoles and high-heeled vinyl boots in elementary school, as long as they make you happy? Plenty.

> *Remember when . . .*
> Gentlemen were embarrassed to use vulgur epithets when conversing with ladies—instead of *learning* vulgur epithets from conversing with ladies?

Slovenly attire, vulgar language, and ads on TV that counsel you on what to do in the event of a four-hour erection are now blandly accepted. I'll never forget the time my father had to entertain a business associate from a large paper company. In enumerating his company's products, our guest listed "sanitary products." Sitting right in our living room! Of course nobody batted an eyelid, but Mama later explained that unfortunately my father would not be able to sever ties to the paper company because he had to make a living. In contrast, Thomas Bertonneau, writer and college English professor at SUNY-Oswego, told me about the young man who wore a "He Farted" T-shirt to class—an arrow pointed wittily to one side. "I see quite beautiful coeds walking in the corridors," adds Bertonneau, "and every other word out of their mouths is the F-word." In my day, our mothers were adamant—never, never, never use the word s-t-i-n-k. Somehow, they neglected to caution us against the F-word.

An English professor at Emory University in Atlanta recounts similar experiences. "Last year, in my freshman class on print and digital media, we had a discussion about the F-word," writes Mark Bauerlein in a 2012 article in the *Chronicle of Higher Education*, "and I was astonished to hear two of the brighter students in the class arguing for its use as a singularly expressive token. When I raised the issue of propriety, they claimed that any stigma was just a generational thing, and that when their generation matures, the F-word and other expletives will have normal status."

Students of Arnold Toynbee will readily recognize what is going on here. In a famous chapter of his *A Study of History* entitled "Schism in the Soul," Toynbee wrote that it is a sign that a society is disintegrating when it takes its cues for manners and customs from the underclass. Toynbee describes such societies as being "truant" to their own values. The British historian may have had been a trifle stuffier than your average American—he regarded an apache scarf on a public school lad in the 1940s as "proof positive that the proletarian style

An Early Exemplar of White Trash Normal

"The demeanor of [the Roman emperor] Caracalla was haughty and full of pride; but with the troops he forgot even the proper dignity of his rank, encouraged their insolent familiarity and, neglecting the essential duties of a general, affected to imitate the dress and manners of a common soldier."

—from Edward Gibbon's *History of the Decline and Fall of the Roman Empire*, as quoted by Toynbee

was à la mode"—but he does describe what we see around us today.

While waiting in the emergency room with a child, you are almost inevitably treated to Jerry Springer reruns. How do you explain "Honey, I'm a Ho" or "Transsexuals Attack!" to a tot? Oh, wait, maybe the tot explains them to you! Alas, fisticuffs are likely to break out as the result of unwelcome paternity test results. Journalist Naomi Schaefer Riley wrote recently in the *New York Post* of being unable to shield her two small children from the sight of huge, borderline pornographic ads on a Metro platform. The ads, part of a campaign for Equinox gym, included one featuring an entwined, scantily garbed couple and was captioned "Rejuvenation." "The idea behind this shot was that the couple was recuperating after sex," a spokesman for the campaign told *Women's Wear Daily*, "so I had to keep reminding [the photographer Terry Richardson] that we were going for a 'post-coital' feel. He just started yelling, 'Post-coital! Post-coital!' with every pop of the flash!" Charming.

While there was widespread outrage over New York subway ads designed to reduce teen pregnancy, nobody seems to have batted an eye over the Equinox ad campaign. But why would they? "Thanks to the ubiquity of pornography, an image that might have raised objections fifteen years ago no longer does because everybody knows it's tame comparatively speaking," Mark Regnerus, author of *Premarital Sex in America*, told Schaefer Riley.

Other gyms are disturbing in other ways. Returning to our favorite subject, I note that sports columnist David Whitley is still old-fashioned enough to be put off by tattooed women at his gym. "I still cringe when I go to the gym and see middle-aged women with barbed wire circling their biceps. They have bigger arms than I, so I never make fun. But I can't shake the notion that a person's body is a temple, and you don't cover temples in graffiti," the columnist wrote in 2012. Whitley was actually addressing another new development: the NFL's very first grotesquely tattooed quarterback. Quarterbacks are, as Whitley put it, comparable to the CEOs of high-profile organizations; whatever other players might do, more is expected of quarterbacks. That heretofore included not looking like a parolee. But NFL quarterback Colin Kaepernick, one of the best, had recently emerged into the spotlight with body art "that must make the guys in San Quentin happy." Kaepernick is especially talented. "His ink-covered arms will one day raise the Vince Lombardi Trophy. Imagine the impact that could have," Whitley wrote.

A. J. McCarron, the quarterback of Alabama's Crimson Tide, looks like the clean-cut product of a Southern Episcopal high school that he is—until you notice the earring. I feel certain that young Mr. McCarron is sporting something much nicer than the Moise Men's Urban Tribal Design Hoop Earrings available at Walmart®. But it's the same general idea. Maybe Mr. McCarron will conquer new territory by someday advertising earrings instead of Nikes®? Perhaps I'm being harsh: if so, blame the aging, fedora-wearing hippie gent with an earring and his stringy gray locks pulled back into a sparse ponytail who is an unappetizing sight many mornings as we cue up for morning coffee at the deli. But I am only showing my stuffiness, fixating on something small enough to dangle from a big guy's ear lobe in a world where body piercing is all the rage.

Like tattoos, body piercing has gone mainstream. Can you imagine going for a job interview with spikes protruding from your upper lip? Tongue studs, at least, have the advantage of remaining hidden unless you stick your tongue out. Frankly, I wasn't the least concerned when a young woman of my acquaintance, a bright girl who was accepted by a name-brand college, acquired pink hair; when, however, I learned that she also had pierced an eyebrow and nipple, I grew alarmed (no, appalled). One outgrows pink hair

> *Remember when . . .*
> Girls wanted diamond rings—
> instead of nose rings?

and, while odd for a time, having pink hair doesn't cause bacteria to breed. The same cannot be said for piercings.

Yet despite the hazards, body piercing is now so taken for granted that Fox's Dr. Manny Alvarez featured a segment on the "Do's and Don'ts for Safe Body Piercing" on *Dr. Manny's Health Beat*. Sample tip: Practice good hygiene. On the other hand, "Smoking and drinking alcohol after an oral piercing," are not recommended. Dr. Manny's warnings came on the heels of an eighteen-year-old Indiana woman's loss of a bosom because of an infection caused by piercing. The girl's mother was angry . . . at the piercing shop. They had not specifically asked her daughter if she was a diabetic. Cosmetic surgery has gone from being a rare event handled with the utmost discretion—"Oh, I just got a good night's sleep"—to being almost an addiction, leading to Facelift Exhibitionism. Joyce Wildenstein, whose 1999 divorce from New York and international art dealer Alec Wildenstein made headlines, reportedly spent $4 million on the not entirely successful cosmetic surgery that led to Mrs. Wildenstein's nickname, "Bride of Wildenstein." The apotheosis of Facelift Exhibitionism, however, was a Fox reality show, *The Swan*. *The Swan* featured women who supposedly were ugly ducklings before the services of a battery of plastic surgeons, dentists, and personal trainers, with the before and after being unveiled before the cameras. Think, if you are unkind, of *The Biggest Loser* for ugly people. The show had a brief lifespan in 2004, but don't despair. Word is that Fox is contemplating a celebrity version.

While some of the former ugly ducklings were happy with the results of their well-publicized excursions into cosmetic surgery, others regretted the experience. Beth Lay, a twenty-five year-old customer service representative, had residual numbness caused by her tummy tuck and liposuction, according to a *People* magazine profile of several Swans. "Newly-minted looker" Kristy Garza and her Marine husband wished in the wake of the show they had money for couples counseling. Unlike in the past, men flirted with Kristy and it bothered her husband. Phaedra Alert: Rachel Love-Foster's husband told *People* that the *Swan* experience not only made his wife more beautiful to him but drew her closer to his sons by a previous marriage.

We may believe that doing away with the customs and conventions of a stuffy elite releases creativity and brings about a renaissance. As a rule, this could not be further from the truth. According to Toynbee, self-expression replaces creation when disintegrating societies look downward rather than upward for sources of inspiration. "We mean a state of mind in which antinomianism is accepted—consciously or unconsciously, in theory or in practice—as a substitute for creation," Toynbee wrote, describing the decline of Hellenistic civilization. Antinomianism is a fancy word for the White Trash credo: hit don't matter. If you don't see what I'm getting at, two words: skank stamp. Tattoo is the ultimate in self-expression devoid of creativity. "Some people get their tattoos to both help themselves and to make a statement to others," writes Margo DeMello in *Bodies of Inscription: A Cultural History of the Modern Tattoo Community*. DeMello quotes one man as saying, "[Having tattoos] separates me from anybody else. No one else has anything like what I have. I feel a little bit different from Joe Shmoe in the street, and I guess it makes me feel special." Here is a sad instance of someone's identity being literally skin deep.

Not that everybody who wears a tattoo sets out to be White Trash (or, as case may be with certain tattoos, Lower White Trash). "A lot of my coworkers and the economics faculty that I work with through grants have tattoos," my tattooed friend from the think tank said. "A lot of the economists' tattoos are either economics or liberty-related with slogans such as 'Who is John Galt?' or supply and demand curves." She added, with regard to the Toynbee thesis, "Who's to say that the styles and manners of the lower class might not occasionally be superior to the upper classes?"

Whatever the artistic merit of tattoos—and I'd say it's nil—these modern-day Caracallas are imitating not the "common soldier" but a stratum of society that in the past was not regarded as worthy of the highest form of flattery. "The statistical association of crime with tattooing is stronger, I feel

White Trash Anger Management

While economists with John Galt tats may not see it, antisocial sentiments lurk just under the surface—or just above the surface—of the tattooed population. DeMello reports a college professor's motivation for inking herself:

> I was saying, "Fuck you, school, and I don't really care if you know I have a tattoo." I also at this time started getting pierced because basically I'm taking my anger out on this school.... I knew it would freak them out, which gave me no small amount of pleasure.

certain, than between crime and any other single factor, with the possible exception of smoking," writes Theodore Dalrymple, chronicler of the miserable lives of the British underclass and an implacable foe of tattoos. The heroes of modern tattooing, the pioneers who helped make tattoos acceptable to the middle classes, are people such as Fakir Musafar, the former Roland Loomis, a leader of the so-called modern primitive movement. A shaman to boot, Musafar praised "urban aboriginals" for rejecting "Western cultural biases" by getting tattoos. Samuel Steward, approvingly described as "a sexual outlaw on the gay frontier" in a July 25, 2010, *New York Times* headline, was another pioneer. He was the "official" tattooist of the San Francisco Hells Angels. As a former college professor, Steward was able to bring a certain *je ne sais quoi* to the tattoo project. His prized possession was a pubic hair from silent star Rudolph Valentino. There was nothing bourgeois about *him*.

Much as supposedly sophisticated members of what DeMello calls "the tattoo community" insist that their tattoos are superior to the ones worn by convicts and bikers, the claim doesn't hold up if you visit an upscale tattoo parlor. I paid a visit to Cirque du Rouge, where my friend acquired her distasteful aviary, in the shadow of the Capitol dome. The "artists" there are much sought after, and I'm told that clients must often wait quite a while for an appointment. ("Make you're appointment with time," a satisfied—if grammatically incorrect—Cirque du Rouge customer urges on an internet site.) The "art" in the portfolios of the Cirque du Rouge tattooists is more colorful than prison tattoos but not really that far removed. At a UK tattoo parlor, Dalrymple saw designs

featuring "sub-Wagnerian Norse mythology, the female figures deriving in equal measure from Brünnhilde and Ursula
Andress, the male from Siegfried and Arnold Schwarzeneg-
ger." He also observed skull and snake designs. I can report
that the very same aesthetic holds sway at Cirque du Rouge.
Menacing flowers (I know—it's hard for flowers to be menacing, but these manage it), threatening birds, and vaguely
mythological creatures with elaborate headdresses are popular. Only a generation that has come of age in an era with a
debased aesthetic could consider this tattoo "art" anything
short of hideous. My favorite tattoo story: David Beckham,
the soccer star who is festooned with tattoos commemorating
milestones in his life, had his wife's name tattooed on his arm
in Hindi.

It is misspelled.

White Trash Recipes–
for When You Want to
Eat (and Drink) Like
Hit Don't Make No Difference

White Trash Cocktails
A Drink for Every White Trash Occasion

*m*any thanks to Anne Lloyd, New Orleans chef and cateress extraordinaire, for help with the recipes throughout this book. The beautiful fare turned out by Anne's upscale Nolavore Catering is about as far as you can get from Hamburger Stroganoff Casserole. But Anne was game to help out, and in the spirit of rescuing a hapless author whose signature dish is a mean mayonnaise sandwich, just for a bit she turned her attention from seasonal ingredients and classically inspired recipes to Velveeta® cheese and baking with Twinkies®. The result was brilliant! Kudos to a great cook from a great food town.

Redneck Riviera Iced Tea

Great for taking out on the fishing boat in the morning.

Ingredients:
- 1 ounce white rum
- 1 ounce gin
- 1 ounce tequila
- 1 ounce vodka
- 3 ounces sweet tea
- 1 ounce Coke®
- Lemon wedge

Fill a 16-ounce pint glass with ice; pour in liquors, then tea and coke. Garnish with lemon wedge.

Not-So-Cosmopolitan

A variation on a classic, prepared with White Trash staples.

Ingredients:
- 1½ ounces Everclear®
- 2 ounces Kool-Aid®
- 1 ounce orange Gatorade®
- Lime twist

Fill a cocktail shaker with ice. Pour in Everclear®, Kool-Aid®, and Gatorade®. Strain into martini glass and garnish with lime twist.

Instant Irish Coffee

Doubles as a complete White Trash breakfast.

Ingredients:
- Sanka® or Folgers® Instant Coffee
- 2 ounces Irish whiskey of your choice
- Cool Whip®

Prepare 12 ounces instant coffee in microwave; pour in Irish whiskey and top with Cool Whip®.

Spiked Church Punch

Granny won't know what hit her.

Ingredients:
- 1 liter dark rum
- 1 46-ounce can pineapple juice
- 1 2-liter bottle ginger ale
- 1 half-gallon lime sherbet

Fill a large punch bowl with rum and pineapple juice. Remove lime sherbet from paper container in whole block form and float in punch bowl. Top with ginger ale. Serves 30.

Tab® and Rye

The yo-yo dieter's substitute for rum and Coke®.

Ingredients:
- 1½ ounces rye whiskey
- 3 ounces Tab®

Fill a 12-ounce rocks glass with ice; pour in rye and top with Tab®.

Shotgun Champagne Cocktail

Perfect for those spur-of-the-moment weddings.

Ingredients:
- 3 ounces Boone's Farm® Wild Raspberry
- 2 ounces 7-Up®

Pour Boone's Farm® into champagne glass and top with 7-Up®. Do not stir.

White Trash Whiskey Sour

A drink you can make anytime, anywhere—including in a fast food cup in your car, because you left all your kitchen utensils in your foreclosed McMansion.

Ingredients:
- 2 ounces bourbon
- ½ lemon
- 1 fast food packet (1 teaspoon) sugar

Pour into a cup and stir with your finger.

Chapter Two

White Trash Money Management

*I*f only fatso Uncle Sam would rein in his spending habits the way an average American family does when it makes its budget around the kitchen table, we could balance the budget and pay off our national debt ...

Snap out of it. Who do you think triggered the foreclosure crisis—the Tooth Fairy?

If you google "foreclosures outrageous stories," you'll find that the Tooth Fairy Theory of the late financial crisis has many adherents. Not a single story I was able to find addressed the issue of personal responsibility. "Even Academy Award winners are suffering from financial woes this recession," began a 2009 story on CNN Money. The "foreclosure victim," as he was dubbed, was Nicolas Cage, one of Hollywood's top earners. Poor Mr. Cage had just lost four houses to foreclosure: two in tony neighborhoods in New Orleans, one a famous Bel Air residence, and another an expensive house in Las Vegas (please, no *Leaving Las Vegas* jokes). Drat those tooth fairies! Call me crazy, but isn't a rich movie star expected to keep up the mortgage payments on at least one of his fabulous houses?

Couples seem genuinely not to understand their part in the tragedy when their houses—with the media rooms, giant columns, and twice as many bathrooms as occupants—are sold from the courthouse steps. Before that happens, many simply up and leave. There are

> *Remember when . . .*
> "Owning" a house meant it belonged to you . . . not the bank?

even "walk away" firms to help defaulting borrowers with the process of reneging on their mortgages. Once this would have been a cause for eternal shame. Today some seem to regard it as virtuous. A 2011 Huffington Post story on "Learning to Walk" quoted one satisfied deadbeat. "We get daily calls from creditors and banks that threaten this and that, and I just laugh knowing I am helping to bring down the system that has brought us all down and continues to reap giant profits at the expense of the little guy." The "hostility people felt from the banks" made walking away easier for others. Imagine that—a bank that wants you to pay your loan! I'll bet that even George Bailey didn't think it's such a wonderful life that it's okay for people to ignore their obligations without extenuating circumstances. (Wanting a McMansion is not an extenuating circumstance.)

"We liken financial behaviors today to where drugs and sex were five or 10 years ago," Joyce Serido of the Norton School of Family and Consumer Sciences told the *Arizona Republic* in 2011. Just a few sobering facts: A student who graduated from college in 2012 owed on average $18,900 in college loans, as compared with $9,000 for a 1992 graduate. We as a nation have loaded up on $800 billion in credit card debt. A stunning number—40 percent—of Americans relied on plastic to pay basic living expenses such as food or shelter in 2012.

Remember the Clampetts? Jed Clampett and his family on the popular 1960s TV sitcom *The Beverly Hillbillies* struck it rich and actually paid for their swanky digs in the Hollywood Hills before they moved into them. For all their funny ways, the Clampetts were models of financial probity. So despite being hillbillies, they were not White Trash. Wish I could say that for the majority of my fellow Americans.

Today, by contrast, millions of Americans who started out in life with far more "advantages" than the fictional Clampetts live their lives a few steps ahead of the bailiff: they take out loans to buy fancy houses they can't afford, rack up credit card debt, and when they finally can't cough up the money for the mortgage, flee, leaving behind swimming pools and granite kitchen counter tops they should never have "bought" in the first place. Indeed, if the rusting pick-up truck on concrete blocks in the front yard is the symbol of Old White Trash, then the symbol of New White Trash is the deserted, mosquito-infested swimming pool in an upscale neighborhood. The Clampetts would have been ashamed to behave in such a fashion.

White Trash Money Management is a subject near and dear to my heart: my editor has told me that—no matter the shame—I must make a confession. When it comes to money management, I am recovering White Trash. I was born Shabby Genteel, which means that you can go either way with regard to money management. My mother chose the path of rectitude. In her entire life she never bounced a check or made a late payment. I, on the other hand, chose the path of—um—less rectitude.

Many a time I enjoyed a purchase that was more expensive than the price tag because of the Non-Sufficient Funds fee tacked onto the purchase. Oh, I'll pick up the check (or maybe another member of the family would like to?), I always told myself. I did always pay, but

Old White Trash
Going to jail for moonshining

New White Trash
Going to jail for a "liar's loan"

Old White Trash
A low standard of living

New White Trash
A high standard of living you can't afford

Old White Trash
Rusting pick-up truck on concrete blocks in front of your tar-papered shack

New White Trash
Mosquito-infested swimming pool in back of your foreclosed McMansion

today, older and wiser, I shudder to think about my $36 egg-plant from the corner grocery. The main problem, as I then viewed it, was that holding a fulltime job would interfere with my literary aspirations. My ploy when I was in my twenties and broke was to regularly pawn Great Aunt Fannie's engagement ring. I kept telling myself that Mr. Diener was the *society* pawnshop. But let's face it: going to the pawn shop is White Trash. There is no way around it, whether you're pawning Uncle Buck's gee-tar or Aunt Fannie's diamond. On top of that, I sat down one day and did the math. That was the last time I ever pawned Aunt Fannie's ring.

The best example of a White Trash escapee I've ever heard of is my friend Jeannette Walls, author of the mega best seller *The Glass Castle.* Jeannette, who is the most sophisticated person I've ever known, actually grew up poor, on occasion even scavenging for food in the high school garbage bin. But she took a bus to New York, got a job, and put herself through Barnard College. At one point, Jeannette was taking a hot bath in her walk-up flat in New York when she had an epiphany: if you get a job and pay the bills, they won't turn off your electricity. After my last trip to Mr. Diener's I had a similar epiphany: if you get a full-time job and never bounce a check, you'll have plenty of money to meet expenses. So I got a regular job with a newspaper, which was the beginning of a whole new life. You can ask my banker, I am a model citizen. And the odd thing is that it isn't that difficult.

There are, I thus adduce, two keys to not being White Trash: having a job and paying your bills on time. The first is getting more difficult in this economy, but it is still White Trash to go on disability if you aren't positively unable to lift a finger.

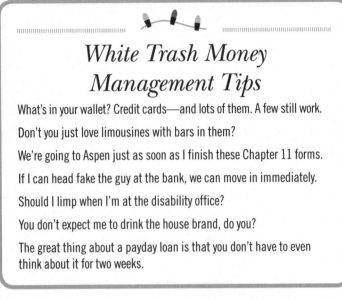

White Trash Money Management Tips

What's in your wallet? Credit cards—and lots of them. A few still work.

Don't you just love limousines with bars in them?

We're going to Aspen just as soon as I finish these Chapter 11 forms.

If I can head fake the guy at the bank, we can move in immediately.

Should I limp when I'm at the disability office?

You don't expect me to drink the house brand, do you?

The great thing about a payday loan is that you don't have to even think about it for two weeks.

A good way to judge the financial stability of a family is its ability to cope with a sudden emergency. A study of "financially fragile families" for the Brookings Institution in 2011 found that about half of U.S. families were not confident that they could muster $2,000 (about the price of a major car repair or co-pay for surgery and a stay in the hospital) within thirty days. Nineteen percent would meet the challenge by taking drastic actions such as pawning or selling possessions or taking out payday loans.

It is easy to sympathize with a low-income family that might find it impossible to raise the money. Such a predicament would be a cause for sympathy and, if possible, a nudge towards finding reputable assistance and good financial advice, especially if the family has children.

But it wasn't just low-income families that were not confident they could handle the emergency. "The...surprising finding is that a material fraction of seemingly 'middle class' Americans also judge themselves to be financially fragile," the study found. One out of four of families with incomes in the $100,000 to $150,000 range didn't think they could raise $2,000 in thirty days!

With apologies to Jeff Foxworthy, if you earn six figures and don't have a rainy day fund, you are officially White Trash. It is important to get one thing straight: being poor is not what makes anybody "trash." Hard-working janitors and waitresses who are raising their children to have good values are anything but trash. Indeed, they are role models who show us by example that reaching for the American Dream is a slow and painstaking process. What we are talking about is something else: people, often quite wealthy ones, who do trashy things with their money. A house you can ill afford is not a sign of good taste and discernment. Neither is credit card debt. The credit card, a fine thing in the hands of a careful person, is a particularly dangerous trap—it's possible to grow an originally small debt into a large one by extending the payment over years. In 2006, Americans paid more than $17.1 billion in late fees to credit card companies.

When the housing bubble burst partly because too many people had "bought" houses with loans they could not repay, the newspapers were full of what I like to call "foreclosure sagas." As a long-time renter, I must confess these mawkish stories left me cold. And the stories were curious: the disasters were inevitably portrayed as something that had just fallen out of the sky. 'Sup? Oh, I can't pay my bills. Bafflement best characterized the evictees.

People on the brink—or over the brink—of default on a loan were inevitably presented sympathetically, as passive and ineffectual. Of a man facing imminent foreclosure on a house near Atlanta, Georgia, on which he had taken out a $416,000 loan—and that's a lot of house for a Southern city in 2006—a usually hardnosed *Washington Post* columnist mistily noted, "The 40-year-old father of four was only thinking about his family. He just wanted to do better for them." I don't want to be judgmental, and I can imagine how scary the situation was, but still one might think that doing better by one's family would exclude signing on the dotted line for a ruinous home loan. It is, after all, a good idea to review one's finances before taking out a loan. The columnist suggested that one would be wrong to assign blame because "lenders were handing out home loans like Halloween candy." Even so, aren't you supposed to do some arithmetic and perhaps say, "Gee willikers, I don't think I can afford this danged mansion"?

> *Remember when . . .*
> People saved for a rainy day—
> and their houses didn't end up
> "underwater"?

But too many people didn't do that. There was a strange disconnect between financial decisions and their almost certain consequences, a fecklessness once associated only with an underclass.

White Trash Euphemisms

In the foreclosure crisis, it became customary to speak of houses that were decreasing in value—as the borrower struggled (or didn't) to make payments—as being "underwater" or "submerged," as if failing to make good on a loan were the result of an act of God: it rained and I couldn't pay my bills. As Toby Keith sang on an album titled, interestingly enough, *White Trash with Money*:

> Yeah, we'd save it all up for a rainy day but it's always sunny
> Guess all the happiness in the world can't buy you money.

We heard a lot about "predatory lending" as these stories unfolded. But wait a minute. Did the lender hogtie an innocent victim and force a signature at gunpoint? Sure, there are people who, often tragically, fall for scams. There are people who send money to Nigerian bank accounts. But for the most part, borrowers who reneged on their loans were people who either hadn't done their homework or had quite simply decided— what the heck—*I want this*. It's more fun to hate bankers than to hold people responsible and call them on trashy—and in fact predatory—borrowing. "It takes two to tango," says Alex J. Pollock, former president and CEO of the Federal Home Loan Bank of Chicago, now a resident fellow at the American Enterprise Institute, "and it takes two people to make a loan. The borrower must ask, 'Can I afford what I am getting into or not?'"

Job loss, it should be noted, is a genuinely mitigating factor for losing a house, as it always has been—a job being the key to getting into and remaining in the middle class. (For the record: I hate this constantly dividing us into classes.) But all too often these victim borrowers, as they were portrayed by a sympathetic press, were not victims of fate. They were the captains of their financially rickety ships, victims of nothing more than their own lack of self-discipline. "What always happens," says Peter Wallison, Arthur F. Burns Fellow in Financial Policy Studies at AEI, "is that people start looking for a place they can afford, and the agent says, 'I can show you another place a little bit better and provide financing.'" Wallison, unlike the press, is old-fashioned enough to realize that, even if dazzled by a vaulted great room, you should check your finances before buying. Many shaky borrowers were speculating—gambling—that the prices of the houses they could not afford were going to go up or, in the words of Toby Keith, that it would always be summer. They just couldn't rein in their desire for a big, swanky house.

The media, which still sets the agenda for the popular culture, however, has a different message about these deadbeats: It isn't their fault. Let's not be harsh. Some people got in trouble because of circumstances beyond their control, but the press and the government said in effect: don't you dare hold any of these people responsible. The government did it with bailouts for bad borrowers at taxpayer expense, while the media wrote mash notes to deadbeats. In this way, two powerful segments of society conspired to positively beg people to act irresponsibly and thereby promoted White Trash Normal.

One of the most shocking borrower-victim stories in the press wasn't about a mere deadbeat. The subject of this column was a man who had gone further, taking out what came to be known as a "liar's loan." For those of you who have yet to obligate yourselves for a $3,000-a-month mortgage on a $3,555 monthly income, the liar's loan is easy to define: you lie to get it. But *New York Times* financial writer Joe Nocera found much to like in Charlie Engle, then residing behind bars. A tape of Engle obtained by somebody wearing a wire ("unbeknownst to Engle"—as if some wire wearers make the wire knownst to the subject!), caught Engle saying, "I had a couple of good liar loans out there, you know, which my mortgage broker didn't mind writing down, you know, that I was making four hundred thousand grand a year when he knew I wasn't."

> ║║
>
> ### *Remember when...*
> "Liar" was a personal insult—not a kind of mortgage?
>
> ║║

Well it takes two to tango.

What is so fascinating about this column is not Engle's plight but where the sympathies of a columnist for the nation's paper of record lie—solidly with Mr. Engle. Needless to say, Nocera is not in favor of lying, but nevertheless he reserves his harsh judgments for the rats who put Engle in prison. Why, they even resorted to "dumpster diving" to get incriminating papers! The columnist finds Engle "easy to root for"—and he does plenty of rooting, including providing some unconvincing evidence in favor of Engle's innocence.

A long distance racer pictured hiking on Half Dome in Yosemite Park in better days, Engle is "personable," kicked a serious drug habit, and—call Mother Teresa!—raised money

> *Remember when...*
> Lying for financial gain used to be known as "fraud" and its perpetrators as perps—not victims, or even heroes?

for a charity that brings clean water to Africa through his racing that was, in turn, financed by fraudulent loans. Why, Engle has even been in a documentary on the Sahara produced by Matt Dillon! All in all, this is the sort of guy that our grandfathers would have crossed the street rather than shake hands with. But those were the good old days. Nocera writes,

> "Every experience in life has the ability to teach lessons if I am open to them," [Engle] wrote on a blog as he prepared to enter prison.

How can you not like someone like that?

Confronted with Charlie the charmer, I'm betting the loan officer never had a chance. It was Engle's father, incidentally, who appears to have gotten in touch with Nocera. I'm betting that doting dad didn't send young Charlie Boy from the dinner table without dessert whenever the lad was caught in a whopper. One interesting fact: the Congress passed Dodd-Frank, a cumbersome package of regulations, to cope with the mortgage crisis, but as AEI's Pollock points out, there is one concept that never appears in the legislation's two thousand pages—personal responsibility, which is the key to rising honestly in the world.

Before White Trash became the New Normal, Americans were judgmental about the Charlie Engles of the world. They scrimped for years to buy houses and endearingly often thought of their houses more as their homes than as ATM machines.

Old White Trash

Having eleven undernourished children

New White Trash

Having eleven credit cards you make only the minimum payment on every month

It now sounds positively prelapsarian, doesn't it? Thrift, self-denial, and a sense that one must plan for the future went into financial decisions, at least for upstanding citizens. Americans believed with Ben Franklin that "He that lives upon hope will die fasting." Your status in life was once closely tied to your propensity for work and for meeting your obligations.

As much as I argue for personal responsibility, I have to say that the old system didn't collapse without help. Nope, Uncle Sam, increasingly an old meddler, gave it a shove. In an attempt to give more people access to credit, the federal government made it easier to borrow, reducing income requirements, especially for low-income Americans—the very ones most likely to be harmed by onerous debt. Increasingly across the financial spectrum loans were being made to people with bad credit. As a result of government policies, people were lulled into believing that they were doing the right thing by borrowing beyond their capacity. Sure, in a world without original sin, people might have turned up their noses and resisted taking out bad loans. But temptation is temptation, and in this instance Uncle Sam became the tempter. He also became the absolver of guilt.

When the federal government bailed out troubled home "owners" to the tune of $26 billion in hard-earned taxpayer dollars, it was presented in the press as help for people over-burdened through no fault of their own. Charles Gasparino of the *New York Post* was a rarity in referring to the benefi-ciaries of the help more accurately as "deadbeats." The justi-fication for the bailouts was that there had been technical errors by some banks in the foreclosure process. Gasparino's refusal to misallocate culpability was bracing. "It's hard to imagine," he wrote, "a less-deserving group of victims: people who gambled during the housing bubble by purchasing homes with borrowed money that they knew or should have known they couldn't afford, but who are now able to stay in the homes they should have never bought because of what amounts to paperwork errors on the part of the nation's big banks." In the past, there was a word for people who didn't pay their bills: White Trash. If there were a Wharton School of White Trash Money Management, its motto would be "hit's not my fault."

In the old days, the coal miner might—as the song went—"owe [his] soul to the company store." More and more college graduates today owe their souls to college loan lenders. Indeed, they have been dubbed "Generation Broke." They find themselves sandwiched between high unemployment and student loans, now the country's largest form of consumer debt. College loan debt has now surpassed the $1 trillion mark. One headline called recent college graduates "the New

Debt Slaves." The most illogical college loans are the so-called "private student loans," taken out to attend such for-profit institutions as the University of Phoenix, a large outfit with more

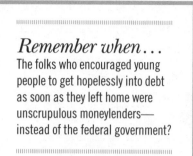

Remember when...
The folks who encouraged young people to get hopelessly into debt as soon as they left home were unscrupulous moneylenders— instead of the federal government?

than two hundred campuses. These institutions are relatively inexpensive but a loan, with interest, may turn out not to be. Saving up or night school might be the better option.

In a way, though, one can see why kids at the ripe old age of eighteen get themselves trapped into what can be life-altering debt. They've been sold a bill of goods. After all, it was the youth idol himself—Barack Obama—who in his first speech before a joint session of Congress said that "education is no longer a pathway to opportunity, it is a prerequisite." So here's what happens: in order to ensure that they will be middle or upper middle class, young people take out loans that may very well ensure that they will not live out their lives in the middle or upper middle class. To get ahead, they get behind. Adding insult to injury, some students—like home loan borrowers—adopt a laissez-faire attitude to the unpleasantness of having to actually repay a loan. Defaults are now at 11 percent, indicating that a large segment of the rising generation has the morally debilitating experience of being deadbeats before they hit thirty. If there is a better instance of the White Trashing of America than our system of college loans, I can't think of it.

Or maybe I can. The idealists of Occupy Wall Street, the short-lived populist movement that erupted in 2011 and gave us public urination, late night drum-beating in residential neighborhoods, and knocking old ladies to the ground, put forward another idea. The movement, it might be mentioned, included a disproportionate number of college kids and indebted recent graduates. *National Review*'s Rich Lowry noted the presence of a man with a master's degree from Harvard and indebtedness of $60,000. He was working at a temp job—which, of course, had some advantages over a nine-to-five job, most notably the freedom to spend endless hours protesting in filth-strewn Zuccotti Park in Lower Manhattan.

> *Remember when...*
> Graduating from college meant you *didn't* end up sleeping in the park?

Occupy, a movement embraced by the president, put forward a simple solution to the troubling problem of college loan debt: hey, dude, forgive it. President Obama, as you might guess, favors more subsidies for college loan programs. But the government has already been subsidizing college loans. This is part of the problem. "By subsidizing student lending, the government has proven that if you subsidize something, you get more of it," wrote Hadley Heath of the Independent Women's Forum. It is interesting that 24 percent of families say that college isn't affordable, but 97 percent believe it is necessary for financial success. But there are creative solutions. Arthur Brooks, president of the American

Enterprise Institute, wrote a famous piece in the *New York Times* headlined "My Valuable, Cheap College Degree." Brooks earned a degree from Thomas Edison State College in Trenton, New Jersey, a virtual college without residence requirements that cost him $10,000. Brooks took correspondence courses from several colleges, including the University of Washington and the University of Wyoming.

Snobbery—always expensive, as Becky Sharp could tell you—is probably behind opposition to such college degrees. Darryl Tippens, the provost of Pepperdine University (one of the most expensive colleges in the nation, by the way), thinks such long-distance learning lacks "the surprise, the *frisson*, the spontaneous give-and-take

> *Remember when...*
> Students used to work their way through college...instead of putting themselves in hock to Uncle Sam for the remainder of their natural lives?

of a spirited, open-ended dialogue with another person." Brooks counters: "My undergraduate years may have been bereft of *frissons*, but I wound up with a career as a tenured professor at Syracuse University, a traditional university. I am now the president of a Washington research organization."

As for the *frissons*, today's college student may be embarking on a life of penury in order to sit—frissonly—not at the feet of the successors of Abelard and Plato but of somebody such as Ward Churchill, the University of Colorado at Boulder professor of "ethnic studies" who called those who perished in the World Trade Center "little Eichmanns." Who needs it?

Not Worth Getting into Debt For

I was recently sent an article by a man who teaches a course on Southern humor (ha ha ha) at his state's premier university. The author pointed out that previous scholars of the subject had failed to examine Southern humor "either as a geopolitical construct, a discursive regime, or a narrative trope." People are embarking on lives of serious debt for courses like this!

Recent college graduates carry an average $3,262 in credit card debt, an increase of 134 percent since the mid-1990s, according to a report from Demos, the liberal policy advocacy organization. Non–White Trash money management tip: take a couple of semesters off and pay off your credit cards.

Thanks in part to our snobbish elite, many people are overlooking lucrative jobs that don't require a college degree. Our elites, in foisting their decadent values on us, have overlooked the wisdom of thrift-meister Ben Franklin: "He that hath a trade hath an estate." He that hath such an estate is unlikely to end up adopting underclass morals and mores. One final word on our costly education follies: I recently rode with a taxi driver who was bitter that he had a degree in economics from the University of the District of Columbia and yet was driving a taxi. His solution to what he perceived as a grossly unfair situation? Go back to school and take some more courses. Perhaps a logic class this time around?

One of the reasons so many people are living like White Trash is—ironically—we are spoiled. We want granite counter tops, new cars, and houses we can't afford. President

Obama said during his 2013 State of the Union address that nobody should work full time and still live in poverty. Sounds good, but I wonder what the colonists at Jamestown or Plymouth would have thought if somebody had told them that. They knew you had to work full time—and then some—and maybe still do a little starving. The upshot was, through thrift and good habits, they prospered. If we don't cure our White Trash ways, we as a society are going down. As the famous cartoon character Pogo liked to observe, "We have met the enemy, and he is us."

White Trash Recipes–
for When You Want to Eat (and Drink) Like
Hit Don't Make No Difference

White Trash Appetizers
As Easy as They Are Depraved—and Just as Tasty

White Trash Snack Mix

Quadruple this recipe to serve 30+ guests at your farewell-I'm-off-to-the-state-penitentiary party. Alternatively, a single batch should see you through an afternoon spent catching up on all those TiVoed® reality shows.

Ingredients:
- 1 1.69 ounce bag M&M's®
- 1 1.74 ounce bag peanut M&M's®
- 1 10-ounce can mixed nuts
- 1 cup Corn Chex® cereal
- 1 cup Rice Chex® cereal
- 1 cup Cheerios® cereal
- 1 cup mini pretzels
- 12 ounces white chocolate chips

Combine all ingredients except white chocolate chips in a bowl. Heat chips over a double boiler until melted. Pour over combined ingredients and mix thoroughly. Spread mixture onto a cookie sheet covered with parchment or wax paper. Let cool 30 minutes, then break into chunks. Store in an airtight container. Serves 8.

Pigs in a Blanket

No, we're not talking about Billy Bob and Rae Ellen when they take a mental health day.

Ingredients:
- 1 can crescent roll dough
- 3 5-ounce cans VYE-eenna sausages
- Lack of good taste

Preheat oven to 375°F. Open can of dough. (Don't you just love to hear that pop?) Unroll dough onto a cutting board. Separate dough triangles from each other, and using a knife, slice each triangle into three smaller triangles. Starting at the wide end of each triangle, place your VYE-enna sausage on top and roll up to the point. Throw the extra three pieces of dough on the kitchen floor for the dog. Place on a cookie sheet with the point side down, then bake for 12–15 minutes or until golden brown. Remove and serve hot with yellow mustard.

Corn Puppies

The *pièce de résistance* for passing at the reception when first cousins marry.

Ingredients:
- 8 strips bacon
- 1 cup cornstarch
- 1½ cups corn meal
- 3 cups all purpose flour
- 8 tablespoons sugar
- 2 teaspoons salt
- 1 tablespoon baking powder
- ½ teaspoon baking soda
- ½ teaspoon cayenne pepper
- 4 eggs
- 2 cups buttermilk
- 1 package hot dogs
- 30 4-inch bamboo skewers
- Vegetable oil for frying
- Yellow mustard for dipping

Fry bacon in a skillet and let cool. Put cornstarch on a large plate and set aside. Fill a pot for frying 3 inches deep with vegetable oil and heat to 350°F. Dice bacon finely and set aside.

In a medium bowl, combine flour, corn meal, sugar, salt, cayenne, baking powder, and baking soda. Make a well and add eggs and buttermilk, whisking into the dry ingredients. Stir in diced bacon.

Cut hotdogs in thirds and pat dry. Roll in corn-starch to coat, shaking off the excess, then skewer each hot dog section with a bamboo skewer. Dip sections into batter one at a time and gently lower into frying oil, working in small batches. Fry until golden brown, then drain on paper grocery bags. Serve with yellow mustard. Serves 8.

Chapter Three

Letting It All Hang Out—
Literally

*I*f the potential demise of the Hostess Twinkie® sent you into a deep depression, chances are you are White Trash.

As Steve Berger observed in his essay collection *Raised by White Trash*, "There's a close correlation between white trash family love and diabetes."

White Trash cuisine tends to rely heavily on carbs, lard, and sugar—all of which have their place when used in moderation. Processed foods are also pillars of this cuisine. What kind of fool cooks from scratch when there are so many attractive processed offerings now available? Got Velveeta®? And remember: Vienna sausages are pronounced VYE-eenna.

Spoiler Alert: If you are expecting a full-throated attack on fast food, stop reading now. Maybe it is (as my mother would maintain) my genes from "the other side" that have given me an abiding taste for foods that the etiolated Arugula Tribe deem hopelessly low rent. But there it is—the first thing I want when I get to Memphis is a Backyard Burger. Cracker Barrel® fried chicken livers = ecstasy. I have a Yankee friend who was just about ready to launch a raid on the zoning board when he learned that a Popeye's® was going up near his house on Capitol Hill. "So much grease," he sighed. "Bliss," I sighed back. For the record: I have many thin friends who are not above the occasional spicy breast from Popeye's®. I'll lay my cards on the table. My theory of White Trash dining: it's more a matter of *weltanschauung* than of judiciously sneaking the odd VYE-eenna.

When the *Daily Mail* did a story on *Here Comes Honey Boo Boo*, TLC's runaway reality hit about a White Trash family, an anonymous blogger responding to the story referred to the stars as Mama June and her "pre-diabetic spawn." One can quibble with the cruelty of calling Alana (Honey Boo Boo's real name) and her multi-dad band of siblings "spawn" and yet agree that Mama June—the matriarch of the family and still, despite having lost a hundred pounds, a fine candidate for a slot on *The Biggest Loser*—makes unwise nutritional decisions. I have to agree: "sketti" sauce made from ketchup and a tub of margarine is puredee White Trash.

Diabetes is the talismanic New White Trash disease, having replaced pellagra, the Old White Trash disease. If pellagra, a vitamin deficiency, was the medical complaint of the undernourished, diabetes is the plague of the overfed. And diabetes, which can have tragic consequences—and, in fairness, is often a bad joke from Mother Nature rather than proof that the sufferer is a degenerate slob—is on the rise: one-third of the children born in 2000 are expected to be diagnosed with diabetes at some time in their lives. So get ready for the shapeless housecoat— that beloved loose-fitting indoor-outdoor garment that is the White Trash answer to the dressing gown—to be seen more

Old White Trash
Owning cows and being too lazy to make butter

New White Trash
Eating butter to the point where you look like a cow

and more on the streets of our land. Expect tighter skin-tight jeans and stretch pants that stretch further. Style and obesity are not two different subjects. The fatter one gets, the more one is inclined to let it all hang out. Literally.

One doesn't have to be a member of the effete Arugula Tribe to find fault with the dietary habits of Honey Boo Boo and her nearest and dearest. The child is practically addicted to what she calls "fat cakes," packaged sweet snacks. Lemonade in the Honey Boo Boo clan is a sack of sugar with a whiff of lemon. The closest the family comes to eating anything fresh is barbecued roadkill. (Does this make them White Trash locavores?) Oh, and Mama June should probably lay off giving Honey Boo Boo so much Mountain Dew® and Red Bull® to pep her up for beauty pageants. (Honey originally came to public attention on a show called *Toddlers and Tiaras*.) Not surprisingly, Honey Boo Boo, age seven, reportedly went from seventy to eighty-five pounds in a matter of a few months during one season. I'm seeing lots of trips to the local "Continue Care" (the present active participle is a pre–White Trash point of grammar) in her future.

But she won't be alone. If you are as big as the side of a barn—to use an expression that has probably been outlawed by the sensitivity police—don't blame my beloved Popeye's. Becoming morbidly obese is what will inevitably happen if you live by the White Trash credo: hit don't make no difference. More and more people are finding themselves simply unable to eat like ladies and gentlemen—and here, for once, I don't mean picking up the right fork. I mean not eating an ungodly amount of glop. One spicy breast at Popeye's® does not White Trash make. Five servings of flaky biscuits, on the other hand, do. And there are many such among us: 36 percent of adults and 17 percent of children in the United States are obese. We speak of an obesity epidemic; what we mean is that White Trash dining has gone mainstream. In addition to the roughly one-third of Americans who are obese, about another third are overweight.

We look like hell as a nation, and fat people bear a large brunt of responsibility for this. I can remember when going to New York meant seeing beautiful, pencil-thin people in stylish clothes on Fifth Avenue. Where are they now? The other day I saw a fat guy in polyester in my favorite New York restaurant. Sure, it made me feel more like I belonged, but the implications were obvious: the end is near. It has to be acknowledged that standards of personal appearance have fallen across the board. Fat or thin, things aren't what they used to be. Remember hats and gloves for ladies at church

How to Wear the Extra Weight

Whenever one observes travelers in an airport or shoppers at the grocery, the thought must surely intrude: "God must have loved fat people because He made so many of them." Unfortunately, he did not further endow them with a proper sense of what fat people should and shouldn't wear on their soft and copious frames. It is difficult to look soigné if you are overweight, and I have nothing but the highest regard for the well-kempt fat person. William Howard Taft, perhaps history's most famous yo-yo dieter, is my kind of fat man. Our twenty-seventh president always looked well turned out in his voluminous three-piece suits and had such lovely manners that once, during his tenure as Chief Justice of the United States, he gave up his seat on a public conveyance to three lucky ladies. But I am afraid that our contemporary fat people have lost all their pride.

and pocket squares for gentlemen? Some ladies of our grandmothers' vintage thought of going to the grocery without gloves as a form of public nudity. I can remember actually being embarrassed by my dear mother once. We were on a driving trip and made an impromptu stop in Memphis. Mama went shopping at Goldsmith's department store without a hat and gloves. I pretended not to know her. But I date myself.

One of the joys of watching old movies is seeing dapper men who knew how to wear a hat. I was so busy admiring Karl Malden's hat that I almost couldn't pay attention to the strippers in *Gypsy*, which came out in 1962, before we had lost all sense of sartorial propriety. Herbie Sommers may have been den mother to Mama Rose's down-and-out little troop of vaudeville children, but he always wore a starched white dress shirt and nicely tailored suit. Do you miss Jimmy Stewart's debonair camelhair coats and two-button jackets as fondly as I do? Would Fred Astaire have been comfortable dancing in a tracksuit? John F. Kennedy, who did have the decency to wear a nice, sleek top hat to his inauguration, killed hats for men. But the rest of our dress code fell victim to laziness and informality, the key White Trash traits.

Some of our collective weight problem is caused by prosperity. When popular brands of muffins range from 600 to 1,000 calories each, only the vigilant will remain svelte. The National Heart, Lung, and Blood Institute notes that the average bagel sold doubled in size between 1983 and 2003. I guess the operative theory is, "If we bake it, they will eat it." Unfortunately, they got it right. It takes discipline to remain trim in the face of temptation from a jumbo muffin, but it can be done. Obesity rates were stable throughout the 1960s but started going through the roof in the 1980s. I have a theory: obesity rates began their meteoric rise in the 1980s because by that time more and more of us started acting like trash. Maybe most of us aren't quite cooking up "sketti" sauce with margarine, but we are less disciplined than previous generations. More and more families no longer gather for dinner and sit down to a meal and conversation at night.

If my theory is right, then more obesity is to be expected when people buy houses they can't afford, are rude to others, and purchase essentials on a credit card. In short, obesity is a product of a White Trash way of living. Interestingly, a German study that several years ago looked at debt and obesity seems to back up my theory. The study, which had 9,000 participants, found that people who are seriously in debt are two and a half times more likely to be obese, even after adjusting for such factors as income and education. David Krueger, psychiatrist and author of *The Secret Language of Money*, sees a tie between gobbling up food and gobbling up money. "People use food and money in similar ways," Krueger told the *Orlando Sentinel* newspaper. "The driving motivation is: What is going to make me feel better in the next instant? That trumps the better question: What's in my best interest?"

> *Remember when...*
> We ate most of our food at actual sit-down meals with other human beings, and snacks were the rare treat—instead of sustaining ourselves on pre-packaged microwavable concoctions in individual portions?

Obesity, like debt, swells when people don't look to the future—a trait in the past associated with the underclass. The average American carries 2.6 times more debt than he did thirty years ago, according to Federal Reserve Board data cited in the *Sentinel* article. The obesity rate went from about 14 percent to 29 percent between the early mid-1970s and 2000, according to figures from the National Bureau of Economic Research. Debt slobs are often fat slobs. It's downright uncouth. "At every step, the connection between the pleasure of spending and the pain of paying became more segmented," said Krueger. "Plastic cards are like gambling chips," Krueger told the paper, citing a study that found that people using credit cards spend on average 23 percent more than people not using credit cards. People who believe hit don't make no difference eat 23 percent more food than other people. Okay, I made up that statistic.

The government and various do-gooders believe they have a solution to the slob problem: passing new laws to relieve us of the obligation to make wise choices—which, ironically, will only serve to make us *more* trashy. Food nannies such as Mayor Bloomberg have what I call the TSA approach to food: the TSA acts as if it is the liquid shampoo rather than the passenger that is the real danger to the airplane. As they ransack my bag, I reflect that I have absolutely no intention of blowing up the plane. Mayor Bloomberg seems to believe it is the twenty-ounce sugary drink that is the culprit. That the problem is the drinker rather than the drink—that Cokes® don't reach out, grab us, and make us drink them, we grab them—seems never to have entered into his thinking. Some of the impetus for Nanny Bloomberg and his ilk's banning craze is snobbery: how tacky to drink that Big Gulp®. Some of their zeal, however, is justified concern for our collective finances: our medical system spends billions on treating obesity-related health problems. It has been estimated that 10 percent of U.S. medical expenses are related to obesity. Since we don't pay the costs out of our own pockets, we are inclined to believe hit don't make no difference. We are, in other words, health-care slobs.

We would love to pretend that the fat people all around us are just cretins we don't happen to know. But the reality is different. Chubby Honey Boo Boo is the little girl next door for many families that don't have such thick accents that the network thoughtfully supplies subtitles. At the more extreme end of the scale, if you'll pardon the expression, how many times have you seen people actually confined to wheel chairs or scooters simply because they are too fat to walk? But there is a better solution to the slob problem than government regula- tions that won't work anyway. Does Mayor

> *Remember when...*
> The dinner hour was a time for polite conversation—instead of...what dinner hour?

Bloomberg really believe that the Coke® addict is less resource- ful when it comes to getting a fix than the cocaine addict? The answer to our problem may be ... bourgeois values. Bour- geois mothers in the past didn't expect their children to be fed by the schools—at least, not before they were old enough to go to boarding school.

On this my friend the food writer Julie Gunlock, also a wonderfully talented cook and the mother of boys, has the final word. "Many things have been blamed for the rise in obesity among children: sugary drinks and junk food, unhealthy school lunches, Happy Meals®, whole-fat milk, and video games. As such, many feel regulations, bans, and taxes on these items should be pursued," Julie says. "Yet, the best research on childhood obesity suggests something altogether different is the key to keeping kids at a healthy weight.... A 2010 study from Ohio State University found that the solution doesn't lie with government action; it lies with parents devel- oping three simple habits: putting kids to bed early, turning off the television, and eating dinner as a family at least five times a week. None of these activities have anything to do with government regulations. Instead, the solution appears to be parents simply parenting."

If acting like White Trash has made us fat slobs, perhaps the only way to slim down is to act like dull old members of the dreaded bourgeoisie. As with manners, mothers are at least partly to blame when children are overweight—a hard truth to swallow. If we don't want to sink into the earth because we are too fat, we've got to make the sacrifice of adopting shocking bourgeois values. Mama June needs to stop it with the beauty pageants and get Honey Boo Boo a library card. Otherwise, she will get diabetes.

White Trash Recipes–
for When You Want to Eat (and Drink) Like
Hit Don't Make No Difference

White Trash Entrées
Guaranteed to Put More Pressure on That Elastic Waistband

Hamburger Stroganoff Casserole

This recipe has *not* been handed down for generations. Extra selling point: since it doesn't require any wine, you can get all the ingredients *legally* with your EBT card. The potato chip topping gives it a certain *je ne sais quoi.*

Ingredients:
- 2 tablespoons butter
- 1 large onion
- 1 pound ground beef
- ¾ teaspoon paprika
- ½ teaspoon salt
- ½ teaspoon garlic powder
- ¼ teaspoon black pepper
- 2 tablespoons flour
- 1 10.5-ounce can Campbell's® Cream of Mushroom soup
- 1 7-ounce can sliced mushrooms, strained
- 1 12-ounce package egg noodles, cooked and drained
- 1 cup sour cream
- 1½ pound bag Lay's® potato chips, crushed
- 2 tablespoons chopped parsley

Preheat oven to 350°F. In a large pot, sauté onions in butter until translucent. Add ground beef and cook until well done. Add seasonings and flour, stirring to combine. Add cream of mushroom soup and cook on low heat for 10 minutes, stirring occasionally. Add mushrooms and pasta and stir until heated through. Add sour cream and stir until combined, then pour mixture into a casserole dish. Top with crushed potato chips and place casserole in oven for 5 minutes. Remove and top with parsley. Serves 6.

Don't-Get-Squirrelly Brunswick Stew

A White Trash Recipe from more modest times— when even White Trash consumed only what they could afford.

Ingredients:
- 4 pounds chicken thighs (or an equivalent amount of squirrel meat; some people say hit ain't Brunswick Stew if hit don't have a squirrel in hit)
- ¼ cup Crisco®
- 2 medium onions
- 2 28-ounce cans diced tomatoes

- 2 15-ounce cans lima beans
- 2 15-ounce cans corn niblets
- 2 cups water
- 2 teaspoons salt
- ½ teaspoon black pepper
- ½ teaspoon dried thyme
- ½ teaspoon dried sage

In a large pot, heat Crisco®. Add chicken thighs (or squirrel) and sauté 15–20 minutes, turning once during cooking. Remove and let cool slightly. Add onions to pot and sauté, stirring occasionally.

Meanwhile, pull off and discard chicken skin, then separate meat from bone and chop. Return meat to pan and add remaining ingredients. Bring to a boil, then reduce to a simmer and cook one hour. Serves 10.

Bacon Weave Surprise Meatloaf

Surprise! Your cholesterol just skyrocketed.

Ingredients:
- 12 slices bacon (about 1 pound)
- ¾ pound ground beef
- ¼ pound hot breakfast sausage
- 8 ounces Velveeta® cheese
- 1 teaspoon Creole seasoning

Turn one half of an outside grill on to medium heat. Place a smoker box or small skillet with smoking chips over the hot side of the grill. Close the lid and allow chips to begin smoking.

Place a long piece of plastic wrap down on your work area. Line up 6 slices of bacon side by side on top of the plastic wrap, then take the other 6 slices and weave them into the first 6 strips to create a bacon mat. Sprinkle Creole seasoning over bacon.

In a medium bowl, mix ground beef and sausage together. Flatten meat mixture and place on top of bacon until you have an evenly distributed square of meat on top. Cut Velveeta® lengthwise to form two logs. Place them end to end about ⅓ of the distance from the top of your bacon mat. Using the plastic wrap, pull the top edge of the roll down and continue rolling tightly until you have a meatloaf-shaped piece. Discard plastic wrap. Carefully tuck the ends in so that no cheese is visible on either end. Place the loaf on the cold side of your grill and smoke for two hours, replenishing smoking chips as necessary. Remove from grill and allow to rest a minimum of 20 minutes before slicing. Serves 4.

Chapter Four

White Trash Buddhists

s White Trash values have traveled upwards in society, it is not surprising that the tide has engulfed the churches. It used to be that being a Pentecostal or a snake handler in Appalachia made you White Trash. But that's so yesterday. Anyway, you've got to hand it to the snake fellows—they weren't half as ignorant as our nouveau White Trash.

Indeed, I'd bet on the serpent handler any day of the week over my friend—let's call her Jane, and let's just say you'd probably be impressed with her educational credentials—if they could both get on *Jeopardy!* When was the last time somebody had to say to a snake handler, "Bubba, honey, Jesus weren't crucified on Ash Wednesday." Jane resisted at first, but with my silver tongue I finally managed to swing her over to the Good Friday position. She's an Episcopalian.

You do not need an Ivy League degree to be White Trash in your religious orientation these days, but there is no denying that it helps. I am thinking of another friend, a magazine writer who initially thought that Epiphany Church in Georgetown was named after a boutique. He thought this was cool. Then I ruined it by telling him about the Magi.

Walker Percy wrote about being lost in the cosmos, but now we are lost in White Trash America. If—God forbid— you ever fall into a conversation about religion with a stranger, you can just about count the seconds before the dread cliché is dropped: "I don't have anything to do with *organized* religion." This is White Trash religion in a nutshell: proud, ignorant, and messy. Just like in Appalachia—only now it's everywhere! The bon mot about "organized" religion, by the way, is inevitably delivered with an air of superiority. But you know what? Hit's pure White Trash.

A neighbor of mine is a scruffy man with a goatee dyed blue to match his tattoos (yes, I keep noticing them). A dabbler in Buddhism and other Eastern spiritualities—who also belongs to a gay-friendly Episcopal church near Dupont Circle—he has no inkling that it isn't the height of originality when he says, "I just don't like *organized* religion." Apparently, a really disorganized ashram is just the ticket. He adds without a *soupçon* of self-knowledge, "I hope I am not over-intellectualizing this." I set his mind at rest.

Despite the pretensions of its practitioners, all this yoga and ersatz Buddhist spirituality is nothing more than an

updated version of some Snopes floozy in a Faulkner novel
too lazy to get out of her dirty bed in her awful cabin to get
dressed and go to church
on Sunday morning,
while the respectable
Sartoris grandmother
has made sure her grand-
children are scrubbed
and dressed to within an
inch of their lives and
marched them into the
pew to insure that they'll
end up public-spirited
contributing members of
the community. We'll get to the God aspect of religion later.

Old White Trash
Snake-handling on Sunday and
expecting the Rapture to solve
all your weekday problems

New White Trash
Howling at the moon at the
Cathedral of St. John the Divine

Whatever churchgoers believed pre–White Trash Normal—and God knows, my sister and I have wondered many
times what on earth our mother, no scholar, taught her Sunday
school classes—nice people got up, got dressed, and sat in a
pew every Sunday or, if Jewish, on Saturday. (Mosque wasn't
much of an option in Mississippi in those days.) Having a
religious affiliation was part of what made nice people nice.
A by-product of this was at least a glancing familiarity with
ideas and concepts that had built Western civilization. Char-
lemagne? Got him. You could absorb a lot about history and
art just by going to church when I was growing up. On Sunday nights, I frequented St. James Episcopal Church in Greenville, Mississippi, for Evensong and hot teen gossip, not
necessarily in that order. It was when St. James sent us out one
evening, two by two, to help complete a religious survey of

the town that I encountered for the first time a man who
didn't belong to a church.

We kept trying to reframe the question so he'd spill the
beans and let us get back to St. James and scarf down ham-
burgers. In addition to being hell-bound, the poor guy was
clearly starved for attention. We may not have been much of
an audience, two small-town teenagers, but Godless was
thrilled by our incomprehension at his Voltaire-of-the-
subdivision act. When the truth finally sank in, I was shocked—
but not for the reasons he probably—proudly—assumed. I was
already perfectly
aware that there were
people in the world
who didn't believe in
God. After all, we had
tons of books at home
written by atheists,

> *Remember when...*
> Children used to learn Bible
> verses—instead of rap lyrics?

agnostics, and high Anglican priests with Doubts. Indeed, my
own brother-in-law professed to be a non-believer. (Fortu-
nately, he had gone to Sunday school as a child, so we were
able to pass him off as Presbyterian; Mama would have died
otherwise.) But not belonging to a church—well, I never!
What bothered me was not the fate of the man's soul but the
sheer tawdriness of not having a religious affiliation, even a
casual one. Where would his poor kids learn to sing "Onward
Christian Soldiers" or acquire basic (*very* basic, if you happened to be an Episcopalian) knowledge of the Bible?

You may not eat Squirt Cheese on saltines, but if you
don't know at least the first verse of "Oh, God, Our Help in
Ages Past," you may be White Trash. Ironically, it's the old

line WASPs, a people whose very identify is tied to their religious heritage, who have let the team down most. The dear old things may have been a tad dull at times, but they dutifully got their children to Sunday school every Sunday morning before the big Sunday lunch of overcooked roast beef and creamed peas in pastry shells. I'm sure I'm not the only WASP manqué (I later moved on to an even *more* organized church) who has enough Crown and Cross decorations (you got a pin, a wreath, and then a bar for every year of perfect attendance) to cross-dress as a Latin American dictator. But nowadays the churches once frequented by such people are offering yoga classes or *Eat, Pray, Love* study groups in place of Isaac Watts's old hymns. And it is not working. Average Sunday attendance dropped 23 percent for Episcopalians in the last decade, and the Methodists, Lutherans, and Presbyterians have seen similar declines.

Ross Douthat wrote a book entitled *Bad Religion*, which, undoubtedly unbeknownst to Mr. Douthat, is a guide to White Trash religion. "America's problem isn't too much religion, or too little of it," Douthat wrote. "It's *bad* religion: the slow-motion collapse of traditional Christianity and the rise of a variety of pseudo-Christianities in its wake." Often one finds pseudo-Christianity in high places. When the Episcopal bishop of Washington, D.C., steps into the pulpit of the National Cathedral, the premiere church of the Episcopal Church, and reads a poem by New Age poet David Whyte, that's literally Whyte Trash in a once-great house of worship. "It doesn't interest me if there is one God or many gods," Whyte once wrote. "I want to know if you belong—or feel abandoned." Yuck.

You thought the Rapture crowd would believe anything? Wrong. Neo–White Trash religion takes gullibility to a new height. White Trash religion embraces not only pseudo-Christianities but pseudo-scholarship with a simple faith that is almost touching. One of the White Trash notions afoot—and it's among the general populace, not just White Trash academics—is that the early history of the Church is just a one long series of power struggles between men and the women they sought to oppress and impose their odious patriarchal views on. Unfortunately for this point of view, the early Christians were often poor and too busy getting themselves martyred to do much in the way of oppressing women or building up earthly power. St. John the Divine was the only Apostle to reach old age and die in his bed. If there was a power struggle going on, it was with the pagan authorities, not ditzy broads who wanted to dance the Eucharist. The older WASP had some appreciation of this history, but his grandchildren—likely named Apple, Bodhi, and Thor—don't. They were not fortified against such foolishness by the simple expedient of being sent to Sunday school every Sunday. Not sending your children to Sunday school is worse for posterity than having a dead tractor in the front yard.

Some of the new White Trash religions people concoct are parody-worthy but at the same time not a laughing matter. Goddess worship is all the rage, and its devotees fondly believe they are following something quite ancient. But they are deluded. For one thing, they got their goddess all wrong. The girls on the popular '90s TV show *Friends* called on the goddess for help getting dates. Feminist goddess worshippers go

Elmer Gantry Is Dead, but John Dominic Crossan Lives On

One of the mega-selling White Trash classics in recent years is *The Da Vinci Code*, which became a boring movie starring Tom Hanks. Author Dan Brown nimbly had it both ways: hey, it's just a novel, but it's also an attack on the Church. In case you somehow managed to remain blissfully ignorant of this tripe, Christ marries Mary Magdalene and fathers a line of Merovingian kings. You can't make this stuff up. Oh, wait—Dan Brown did make it up. In *The Final Testament of the Holy Bible* by James Frey, "Jesus" tells a Catholic priest, "Love and laughter and fucking are what makes life better." Dostoyevsky this ain't. These books are fantasy for people who are so cut off from their roots that they aren't able to recognize pretentiously packaged junk for what it is. A member of the supposedly high-brow Jesus Seminar, which allegedly searches for the historical Jesus, John Dominic Crossan is a former Dominican friar who has popularized his zany notion—based on no evidence whatsoever—that Christ's body was devoured by dogs after being crucified. That's one way to dispose of the Resurrection! No doubt millions of ignorant people whose lazy parents slept in of a Sunday lap this stuff up as if it had some scholarly basis.

howl at the moon, or some such foolishness, to invoke her. They should count their lucky stars the goddess doesn't appear. Most of the goddesses in the ancient world made Yahweh at his plague-wielding worst look like a pushover. My own personal favorite is Cybele, who insisted that her male worshippers become do-it-yourself John Wayne Bobbitts. I'm told that Cybele has a certain following in transgender circles, and that it is believed that Christianity suppressed her cult because of its "fear" of LGBTQ people. So we should all relax! Why worry if young men are turning themselves into eunuchs for no good reason?

No doubt there are many serious scholars of Buddhism in the West. I am willing to go out on a limb and bet that my neighbor with the blue goatee isn't one of them, however. When my sister was bringing up her sons, she offered bribes if they'd serve as acolytes. The theory was that even if they were little heathens they might get religion later. And if and when they did, she had made sure they would have something solid to fall back on—instead of joining an embarrassing ashram or running off with a maharishi. Nor did she want her daughter to grow up to welcome the solstice in a hot tub. (What she didn't fully anticipate was that the rector of her granddaughter's local Episcopal church would be a divorced lesbian.)

Some other facets of White Trash Normal are just annoying. The elite U.S. press doesn't have the foggiest when it comes to the forms of religion. Whenever there is a ceremony in Westminster Abbey, they get all the clergy titles wrong. Note to White Trash press covering the next royal event in the Abbey: the Archbishop of Canterbury is not called "Reverend Welby." It's not surprising that they don't know the niceties, but it is surprising that they don't know they don't know—and therefore never think to ask somebody.

When Pope Emeritus Benedict XVI wrote a book on the Infancy narratives suggesting the calendar may have Christ's birth a year or two off—hardly a matter of doctrine—the press went wild and had the pope "disputing" the gospel. Not having a nodding acquaintance with religion, they can't

Pseudo-Sophistication at the Paper of Record

The original *New York Times* story about Pope Francis's first Easter blessing contained this gem of reporting, aimed at readers presumed to approach the most basic facts of Christianity with the attitude of the bemused anthropologist encountering the alien customs of primitive savages (not that the *Times* would ever be so rude to primitive peoples—whom they would never call savages): "Easter is the celebration of the resurrection into heaven of Jesus, three days after he was crucified, the premise for the Christian belief in an everlasting life."

Whoops.

Somebody must have pointed out that Easter is *not* in fact about Jesus's "resurrection to heaven." So the amateur anthropologists at the *Times* had to issue this correction: "An earlier version of this article mischaracterized the Christian holiday of Easter. It is the celebration of Jesus' resurrection from the dead, not his resurrection into heaven."

At which point it became apparent that the folks at the *Times* are unfamiliar with the concept of the Ascension, too. (What exactly would a "resurrection into heaven" look like?)

distinguish between what matters and what doesn't matter. Camille Paglia, an atheist art historian who nevertheless has a high appreciation for the beauty engendered by Christianity, has taught students who can't quite place Adam and Eve and haven't the foggiest who that Moses fellow was. "If you are an artist and you don't recognize the name of Moses," Paglia told Emily Esfahani Smith, "then the West is dead. It's over. It has committed suicide."

What these kids needed growing up was a good, old-fashioned Baptist Sword Drill to set them straight. "Sword drills," as my Baptist organist friend puts it, "were something like a spelling bee, but using the Bible—the Sword of the Spirit." The moderator called out something from the Scripture, and the first one to locate it in the Bible stepped forward and read it aloud." It was considered fatal to invite an Episcopalian to church on Sword Drill night because they'd lose for your team. One of my friends was there the night Hebrews was tossed out. She frantically scoured the Old Testament until her Baptist hostess took pity and said, "Meredith, there are lots of Hebrews in the Old Testament, but the *letter* to them is in the New Testament." My sister claims to have cost many a Baptist unwise enough to ask her to church on Sunday nights many a victory in the Sword Drill. But my sister can still recite the Catechism by rote and identify the heraldic shields of all the Apostles, which were prominently displayed in our parish hall. Okay, learning the coats of arms for the Apostles is very Anglican—but you take my larger point: back then we were able to paddle a bit in the stream that is our civilization. We weren't stuck in the hollows.

It is sad that so few children nowadays have the charming experience of memorizing the books of the Bible by singing "Genesis, Exodus, Leviticus" in Sunday school. But then you'd be hard-pressed to find many thriving Sunday schools these days. Like many once civilizing aspects of life, Sunday school is a casualty of divorce. Instead of a morning with Abraham, Isaac, Jacob, and the God of Israel, the modern child is more likely to spend the day visiting the "other" parent. White Trash has always been partial to immediate gratification over long-term planning. Sunday school was the ultimate in long-term planning for the next generation.

Cultural illiteracy breeds White Trash behavior. If you don't know who Adam and Eve were, you probably don't have reasoned arguments as to whether Adam and Steve should get married. Indeed, I'll go out on a limb and predict a day when a clergyman divorces his wife, comes out of the closet, takes a male lover, and then becomes the Episcopal bishop of New Hampshire. Nah, that's crazy. Things will never get that trashy. Sometimes I amuse myself by trying to picture my grandfather, a plain vanilla Episcopalian if ever there was one, "exchanging the peace." No can do. But you know what I really can't imagine? I really can't imagine him—or any of his contemporaries—sitting in a pew at the Cathedral of St. John the Divine engaging in ritual howling. Back in the day, even Episcopalians had a grip on reality.

And, if you think some bumptious coot who dresses like Larry the Cable Guy is full of hisself, you need to get out more. Having grown up mostly without the tempering influence of what was once mainstream religion, today's young are off the charts when it comes to self-esteem, formerly known as vanity. Several recent studies have shown that self-esteem is highest among prison inmates, neo-Nazis, and other assorted bullies. But high self-regard is on the rise among young people in general. Psychologist Jean Twenge's famous study *Generation Me: Why Today's Young Americans Are More Confident, Assertive, Entitled—and More Miserable than Ever Before* looked at the scores on the Narcissistic Personality Inventory evaluation administered to sixteen thousand American college students between the years of 1982 and 2006. The evaluation includes questions such as: "I think I am a special person." "If I ruled the world it would be a better place." "I find it easy to manipulate people." Around 65 percent of the students surveyed in 2006 scored high, a rise of 30 percent from 1982. Can you imagine how scary it would be if one of these narcissists became president? Instead of being puffed up with self-esteem, maybe the young should be learning more about Original Sin.

A beautifully educated young friend of mine possesses a fine mind and is in no way White Trash—except with regard to religion (or lack thereof). He occasionally popped into a mosque when he was required to attend worship services in school, but his contact with his family's religion is minimal. Throwing down the gauntlet to me, he insists that the mention of dragons in Scripture shows that the Bible is nothing but myth. I can only think of how Father Mowbray, the hapless priest charged with instructing the invincibly ignorant Rex Mottram in *Brideshead Revisited*, characterized his charge. "Lady Marchmain," said the despairing Jesuit, "he doesn't correspond to any degree of paganism known to the missionaries." That is the epitaph for our society.

When I attended the graveside funeral service for a friend's aunt, a decade or so ago, we were asked to recite the Twenty-Third Psalm. It was moving to see all the older people, my mother and my own aunt, able to recite the psalm from memory. How much longer will it be possible to ask a congregation to say the Twenty-third Psalm without a printed text? One mustn't think of regular church attendance merely as a way to keep White Trash manners at bay. But it helps.

White Trash Recipes—
for When You Want to Eat (and Drink) Like
Hit Don't Make No Difference

White Trash Side Dishes
There Is No More Enjoyable Way to Give Yourself Type 2 Diabetes

Continue Care Biscuits with Sausage Gravy

Continue Care Biscuits and Gravy make up for coronary damage by melting in your mouth. Larded and lauded! Weight Watchers® points count not presently available.

Biscuits:
- 2 cups all-purpose flour, divided
- 2 teaspoons baking powder
- ¼ teaspoon baking soda
- ¼ teaspoon salt
- 4 tablespoons plus 2 teaspoons lard or Crisco®
- 1 cup buttermilk
- 2 tablespoons melted butter

Preheat oven to 425°F. Set ¼ cup flour aside for kneading. In a medium bowl, mix remaining dry ingredients together with a fork. Scoop in lard or Crisco® and work into the dry ingredients with your fingertips until the mixture resembles breadcrumbs. Make a well and pour buttermilk into the center, then, using a circular motion, work flour mixture into buttermilk until just combined. Turn dough out onto floured surface and knead 10 times only;

dough should just barely hold together. Roll out to ½ inch thick and cut with a 2¼-inch cutter (or a drinking glass turned upside down). Brush a baking pan with half of the melted butter, then place biscuits on pan. Brush the tops of the biscuits with the remaining butter and bake 10–12 minutes, or until tops are slightly browned. Makes 16 biscuits.

Gravy:
- 12 ounces hot breakfast sausage
- 4 tablespoons all purpose flour
- 3 cups whole milk
- 1 teaspoon salt
- ¼ teaspoon black pepper

Heat a cast iron skillet over medium heat. Add sausage and cook, stirring occasionally, until cooked through. Stir in flour until incorporated, then gradually add milk. Season and heat, stirring constantly, until mixture reaches a boil. Turn down to a simmer and cook 10 minutes, stirring often and making sure to scrape the bottom of the skillet.

Slice biscuits in half and arrange on a large platter. Pour gravy over biscuits and serve immediately. Serves 8.

Strawberry Delight Salad

Jell-O® is so versatile! It hits the spot whether you're missing a few teeth because of insufficient dental attention or if you can't chew just now because of too sufficient cosmetic surgery.

Ingredients:
- 1 3-ounce package strawberry-banana Jell-O®
- ½ cup boiling water
- 5 ounces frozen strawberries
- 8 ounces canned crushed pineapple
- 1 large banana, mashed
- ½ cup pecan or walnut pieces
- 4 ounces cream cheese
- ½ cup sour cream
- 1 head iceberg lettuce

Line an 8-by-8-inch baking dish with plastic wrap. In a small bowl, mix sour cream and cream cheese until thoroughly combined. In a medium bowl, pour in Jell-O® mix. Whisk in boiling water, then add strawberries, pineapple, mashed banana, and nut pieces, stirring together. Scoop half of fruit mixture into baking dish. Gently spread cream cheese mixture into baking dish, then spoon remaining Jell-O® mixture on top. Chill a minimum of 2 hours, then invert onto a cutting board, removing plastic wrap. Wash lettuce leaves and arrange on a large platter, then slice fruit delight into squares and arrange on top of lettuce leaves. Serves 6.

When in Doubt, Fry It

A universal fry recipe—because is there anything that doesn't taste better breaded and cooked in grease? This recipe works with onion rings, mushrooms, dill pickle chips, candy bars,* Twinkies® ... and the list goes on!

*If frying candy bars, freeze for at least 2 hours ahead.

Ingredients:
- 1½ cups all-purpose flour, divided
- 1 teaspoon salt
- ¾ cup beer
- ¾ cup buttermilk
- 1 egg
- Vegetable oil for frying
- Items of your choice to be fried

In a medium bowl, combine 1 cup flour and salt. Make a well in the center. Whisk in egg, buttermilk, and beer, incorporating completely.

Fill a frying pot with vegetable oil to 3 inches deep and heat oil to 350°F. Put ½ cup flour in a large bowl and add items to be fried. Toss until coated with flour, then dip in batter, making sure all sides are thoroughly coated. Fry, turning as necessary, until golden brown. Drain on newspaper or unpaid bills.

Chapter Five

Who's Your Daddy?

Dorothy Allison is a novelist who unabashedly describes herself as "white trash." In her semi-autobiographical *Bastard Out of Carolina*, Allison tells the poignant story of Anney, a waitress based loosely on Allison's own mother. As a result of an automobile accident, poor Anney was in a coma when her first child was delivered and thus prevented from telling the face-saving lie that she was married. As a result, the baby's birth certificate bore the word "illegitimate." From then on, Anney's life became a quest to amend the offending document.

So dedicated was Anney to her cause that she set fire to the county courthouse, repository of county records. Anney's pursuit of respectability supplied much amusement for her less fastidious friends and relatives. But it represented an admirable struggle to attain a kind of gentility. Anney had a heartening sense of shame. Would that more girls from affluent families today—many active participants in the "hook-up" culture, belles who, instead of flowers and chocolates on Valentine's Day, enjoy raunchy productions of *The Vagina Monologues*—shared Anney's sense of propriety!

Real-life Anneys today are more likely appear on MTV's popular reality show *16 and Pregnant*. "When you're sixteen and pregnant your life changes," intones host Dr. Drew Pinsky. Unfortunately, not necessarily in the right direction. Whitney Purvis from the first season, for example, was arrested several years after she appeared on the show ... for trying to steal a pregnancy test at Walmart. Whitney and her boyfriend Weston—he was her first boyfriend, who relieved her of her virginity, she explained to the nation on television—had had to live for a while with Whitney's family: her mother, grandmother, and mother's boyfriend Scott. Both mother and daughter were pregnant at the same time.

Old White Trash
Illegitimacy shame

New White Trash
Illegitimacy chic

This is not some niche show that nobody watches. When Amber Portwood—who had a baby girl with boyfriend Gary Shirley—went to prison for using illegal drugs in 2012, the news was reported on ABC in a segment introduced by George Stephanopoulos. Amber, who had chosen to go to prison rather than finish rehab, described her imprisonment as "a situation that has been handed to me." Baby daddy Gary has the little girl, but it can't be easy: the gossip site TMZ reported that while Amber was in prison, Gary was facing eviction from his apartment for not paying rent. Meanwhile, ABC News's Juju Chang characterized Amber's decision to do time as "a chance for this teen mom to grow up for good."

It's not surprising that the girls have a nonjudgmental attitude about their pregnancies. After all, Kim Kardashian, a much richer and more famous reality star, announced that she and rap star Kanye West are expecting a little bundle. Meanwhile, Kardashian's ongoing divorce from estranged husband Kris Humphries continued to grab headlines (at this writing). At issue: Humphries insisted that the seventy-two-day marriage be annulled because, he claimed, the nuptials were merely an excuse for Kardashian to put on a lucrative, televised spectacular. I guess Humphries is the kind of person who passes for an upholder of traditional values today.

If you want to know how far we have fallen since the gloriously uptight 1950s, you need only remember the wedding announcements that used to appear in newspapers. None of the brides in these write-ups were pregnant already, or at least none of them admitted to it. This is not the case with the write-ups that appear in the *Washington Post*'s "In Love" feature, a replacement for the old society section. Less flamboyant than Kim but also less susceptible to shame than Anney, Nicole Alexander and Colin Mitchell, two professionals who wed in 2013, were the subjects of this unblushing paragraph in their nuptial announcement:

> Although they felt fully committed to each other, neither was in a rush to marry. But after Alexander turned 35 in 2011, they began to think about having a family. In October 2012, they took a 10-day vacation in St. Lucia. When the pair came home, they found out Alexander was pregnant. Their baby is expected to be born in July. "It's really a blessing," Mitchell says. "We couldn't have scripted it any better."

Nicole and Colin, if I may call them by their first names, would once upon a time have married quietly, possibly at an undisclosed location, with the wedding followed all too quickly by the birth of a surprisingly large "premie."

Whereas once being a respectable member of society required shotgun weddings, now we hardly notice if the bride has a baby bump. Indeed such weddings are the good news: the bad news is that around 40 percent of births in the United States are to unmarried women. While in Anney's day such births were called

Old White Trash
Having a shotgun wedding

New White Trash
Wearing a designer bridal gown that doesn't hide the baby bump

illegitimate, they are now known more neutrally as "nonmarital." We've also retired the quaint term "born out of wedlock." Heaven forfend if you thought it was trashy for Angelina Jolie and Brad Pitt to be expecting their seventh (as the two humanitarians were at this writing)—and still be nonmarital!

When my older sister was dressing for her wedding in the idyllic 1950s, it suddenly dawned on our mother that she had forgotten something.

"Oh, dear," Mama said to herself, "I forgot to tell Julia about the facts of life." Mama braced herself and cornered

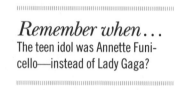

Remember when...
The teen idol was Annette Funicello—instead of Lady Gaga?

Julia, already in her white wedding gown, in her bedroom. "Is there anything you'd like to ask me?" Mama inquired nervously ... Pause ... "Or maybe you'd just rather have a nice Virginia ham sandwich?" Julia opted for the Virginia ham sandwich, and ten months later my niece was born. Julia can still remember the stony face of our rector as he reluctantly shoved a book with a discreet cover across the desk during marriage counseling. Its title was something like *Episcopalians and Sex*. Bet that was a fun read. The marriage worked out just fine, though.

Brides of my sister's vintage made it to the altar without having taken sex education classes in school. Sex education may well be the trashiest innovation in human history. Introduced into public schools in the late 1960s, sex education has always struck me as kinkiness for kids, but many people wax high-minded about the vital importance of teaching young children how to put condoms on bananas.

When I was in high school poetry classes, I honestly wondered why phallic symbols pointed ... oh well, never mind. The premise of sex education, as far as I can tell, is that kids are going to be "sexually active" anyway, and so they urgently need to develop their banana-wrapping technique.

"Low sex-ed literacy results in unplanned pregnancies, sexually transmitted infections including HIV and a lowered well-being for the state's youth," a 2012 New York Civil Liberties Union report claims. According to the NYCLU, the failure to provide adequate sex education was "hobbling [students'] potential for personal and economic growth." In other words, it would be just awful if people had to take responsibility for their choices. But character is precisely that: taking responsibility for one's actions. Not to do so is the epitome of one thing: White Trash. There's no nice way to say this: sex education teaches young people how to behave like trash.

> *Old White Trash*
> A large collection of broken-down vehicles
>
> *New White Trash*
> A large collection of sexually transmitted diseases

And, surprise! "Nonmarital" pregnancies and sexually transmitted diseases skyrocketed in the very years sex education went mainstream. The Centers for Disease Control estimates that there are now 110 million sexually transmitted infections in the American population—that's more than one for every three individuals, though of course the statistics are skewed by the more "sexually active" among us—with 20 million new cases of STDs being acquired every year. White Trash Normal strikes again.

Meanwhile, Think Progress (think regress, in this case?) finds the time to be dismayed by a different statistic: "nearly two in three school districts excluded any mention of female genitalia in their instruction." Thank heavens for small favors! When I was in seventh and eighth grade, we did have some film on "changes in our bodies." It had lots of clouds floating around, and we were so confused afterwards that I doubt if it did any harm. Nobody wanted to go out and experiment because most of us had only the faintest glimmer what was going on. I'm sure a few graphic words about "female genitalia" would have clarified matters.

The proponents of sex ed argue (not particularly convincingly, on the balance of the evidence) that it prevents pregnancies. But here are some things it is undeniably effective in preventing: decency, gentility, good taste, and personal responsibility. I've always argued that sex ed in school is bad because a lousy teacher can ruin a poem. Sex ed teachers, it seems, ruin sex—without making it happen any less frequently. We'd be looked at as if we were Martians if we made the real argument against sex ed: it's in bad taste.

When my sister got married, the entertainment industry's reigning presentation of marriage was the TV show *The Adventures of Ozzie and Harriet*. (I swore I was going to write this chapter without mentioning the Nelsons. But it's not possible.) Ozzie and Harriet Nelson had a wonderful marriage that to this day infuriates feminists. On the show, which ran from 1952 until 1966, the family confronted such dilemmas as whether to turn the boys' bedroom into a game room as they got older and moved away. Harriet opposed the plan for sentimental reasons.

When Ricky and David, the Nelson sons, got married in real life, wives were added to the script. Harriet was the good wife of the fifties and sixties. Her wifely role could not have been more different from that of good wife 2.0, Alicia Florrick (Julianna Margulies), the high-powered lawyer on CBS's *The Good Wife*. Whereas Ozzie Nelson was always leaving home to buy ice cream, Peter Florrick (played by

> *Remember when . . .*
> Americans thought it was normal to be like Ozzie and Harriet Nelson—instead of Ozzy and Sharon Osbourne?

Chris Noth, "Mr. Big" from *Sex and the City*) has left home because of an endless string of adulterous relationships. At one point, Peter, a politician, ends up behind bars; sex was a factor. In the heyday of Ozzie and Harriet, the Florricks would have been seen not as glamorous but as thoroughly trashy. But it's a popular show, and the Florricks are probably a more recognizable American family than the exotic Nelsons would be today.

While Hollywood may think of itself as sophisticated beyond words, illegitimacy chic (a term that came into vogue in the 1980s) in the entertainment world is nothing more than White Trash mores repackaged. C'mon, weren't Woody Allen and Mia Farrow precursors of White Trash Normal? Horny old Woody fooling around with his lover's adopted daughter Soon Yi? More recently—just to hit a few high spots—Halle Berry and supermodel Gabriel Aubrey managed to have a nasty custody battle without ever having been married; Natalie Portman showed up pregnant but not wed at the Academy Awards the year she was nominated for *Black Swan*, and British actress Minnie Driver will not identify the father of son Henry. The late Heath Ledger and Michelle Williams played a married couple on the screen. But they never got around to marrying in real life, despite the existence of a daughter. Sorry, but I can't keep up with the Kardashians. I'd say Appalachia, except that again I don't want to insult Appalachia.

If you are old enough, you may remember *Bachelor Father*, the old TV series. Nope, it wasn't about a guy raising his illegitimate child. Bentley Gregg (played by the elegant John Forsythe) was an uncle bringing up his niece Kelly after her parents died in a car accident. The family includes a devoted "houseboy" (a verboten word today) played brilliantly by Sammee Tong, plus Jasper the dog. A frequent plotline was a search for a woman who might be right for Bentley. In one of the last episodes, Kelly is engaged and nervous about cooking for her fiancé's family.

How quaint it all seems now. The raunchy *Two and a Half Men* is *Bachelor Father* updated for White Trash Normal. The enormously successful show revolved around a feckless, divorced brother living with his son in the Malibu house of a promiscuous older brother, Charlie Harper, played by Charlie Sheen, who enjoys an active and various "nonmarital" sex life despite the presence of an impressionable child in the house. This was Appalachia on the Pacific—again with apologies to Appalachia—until Sheen left the show and careened into his own drug-fueled, real-life version of White Trash Normal.

The behavior of characters on *Two and a Half Men* and other popular shows such as *Grey's Anatomy* (on which, as social commentator Emily Esfahani Smith has noticed, predatory female doctors are always on the prowl for sex in what was once a distinctly masculine—and bad masculine— way) would once have provoked the interest of government censors and the Hays Office (no kin, but sometimes we think just alike). Families that routinely tuned in to watch Bishop Fulton J. Sheen on television would not have been amused by this exchange on *Two and a Half Men*: "What I've wanted to ask you is, do you think I've been a good role model?" caddish Uncle Charlie Harper asks nephew Jake. "Are you kidding?" replies Jake. "You drink, you gamble, you have different women here practically every night. You're the best role model a guy could want!"

As I said, I had hoped to get by without mentioning Ozzie and Harriet. Bringing up the Nelsons is such a cliché—whether you like them, or, as the case may be, deplore the show's depiction of family life. Barbra Streisand, speaking at Harvard, revealed that she preferred *Murphy Brown*, the TV show about a hotshot reporter with a child born out of wedlock. Streisand found that *Murphy Brown* represented "a thoughtful attempt to deal with the reality that Americans now lead lives that, for better or for worse, are different than [sic] the lives of Ozzie and Harriet." Having kids out of wedlock is not trashy in Streisand's view.

True Stories from the Less Trashy America of Yesteryear

An uncle of my own once nearly slipped up and mentioned *in the living room* that the stork was winging its way towards 313 South Washington Avenue, bearing in its beak—me. My distraught grandfather leapt to his feet and began waving his hands in the air. We didn't talk about such things! Even worse was when, a decade and a half later, I was entertaining high school-aged friends in the same living room. I am afraid somebody used the word "commode" that evening. Papa, who had dropped in to say hello, shot out of the room like a cannon ball. Mama, alarmed by the language, felt she could not leave us alone. Nothing like a chaperone who thinks that the word commode is *risqué*. But that's the way it was.

Okay, maybe this was extreme, but I feel certain that I am not the only one of my contemporaries whose childhood home was devoid of potty language. Being Southerners, we were a crazy, intergenerational family under one roof, and we had more loose screws than the Nelson family. But we were more like them than the vulgar Harpers of Malibu. Most families back then, except for the bottom rungs of the underclass, were more like the Nelsons than the trashy Harpers, which is why the Nelsons had such resonance.

Another couple of decades later, I remarked to one of my old friends that it was a good thing, given my stuffy family, that I never "got in trouble." My friend replied, "Yes, it is. Your uncle John would have driven into town and tied your legs together with bailing wire."

She is not alone. Almost half of children under the age of fifteen live in families that are not composed of two biological parents. "As late as 1960, at the height of the Baby Boom, married families made up almost three-quarters of all households; but by the census of 2000 they accounted for just

53 percent of them, a decline that seems to have continued in the past few years," Herbert S. Klein wrote in 2004. A 2002 study by the National Center for Health Statistics found that 61 percent of women in their thirties have lived with a man to whom they are not married. This has to be hard on the children—I wonder if the boorish young people one sees all around aren't products of such households.

When it comes to cohabitation patterns, the United States has become two nations—but not quite in the way the nation's most famous Baby Daddy, John Edwards, also a former White House aspirant, thought: we now have a small, highly educated New Upper Class that has re-embraced marriage—and then we have everybody else. The New Class, which developed in the sixties and originally went in for "living together," is less enthusiastic about cohabitation than it once was for a simple reason: it doesn't work. Marriage is the only way to produce children capable of succeeding. The New Class, however, as the writer Charles Murray has noted, is not judgmental. It still embraces trashy *ideas* about the relations between men and women.

> *Old White Trash*
> Huey Long
>
> *New White Trash*
> John Edwards

New Class couples still object to wife beating (though they do have a yen for a little light sadomasochism; see *Fifty Shades of Grey*), but they have no objection to women boxers, women wrestlers, and women in combat. New Class egalitarians think we're all equal under our tattoos—and each new blow against chivalry is a victory for equality. They think Eve Ensler, who wrote *The Vagina Monologues* has "something important to say." Obama voters by and large, they were not appalled that the president's campaign urged women to "vote like your lady parts depend on it." They were not squeamish when the actress Lena Dunham looked into the camera and urged young women to vote for the president because, "Your first time shouldn't be with just anybody. You want to do it with a great guy.... Someone who really cares about and understands women."

The historian Arnold Toynbee, as you'll recall, pointed out that one sign of a decaying civilization is that it takes its cues on morals and manners from the underclass. From sex ed to the Harpers of Malibu, we are doing just that. It is generally said that the decline of sexual mores and marriage was caused by the revolutionary sixties. That would mean that widespread cohabitation, the death knell of marriage, started with affluent revolutionaries. Poorer people followed suit, though they could ill afford the consequences. Jonathan Last, however, takes a different view—one that sits better with us Toynbee groupies.

In *What to Expect When Nobody Is Expecting*, Last writes,

> If you had to guess where cohabitation came from, you'd probably think that it originated with the countercultural revolutions of the '70s as college radicals turned their backs on bourgeois '50s morality and embraced sexual liberation—and that

this enlightened, sophisticated movement gradually spread to the rest of society.

But the exact opposite is the case. The rise of cohabitation actually began in 1935. It was a slow-rolling wave inaugurated by people without high school degrees shacking up. By 1959, about 18 percent of people under 25 who hadn't graduated from high school were living together. After 1950, their rate shot up to 50 percent in just 10 years and was often higher in the 1970s....

By the time cohabitation hit the college crowd in the 1970s, it was already a fact of life among the lower classes. Seen in this light, cohabitation looks less like an enlightening social change and more like a spreading social pathology working its way up the culture from society's have-nots.

A lack of respect that our grandparents would have had no trouble calling trashy pervades relations between men and women. Whereas we once had chivalry, at least as an ideal, we now have the Violence Against Women Act, which is based on the supposition that men are brutes because of "the patriarchy." The solution: restraining orders that often don't work. The act comes from a mindset that says that men can't be tamed. The law, not the family, becomes the only vehicle for dealing. Believe me, I'm for throwing the book at any man who harms a woman. Whenever there was a news story about a woman killing her husband in the newspaper—and there were several in my childhood—my grandfather would shake his head and murmur, "Poor dear, he probably had it coming."

But I also believe that it starts when the guy doesn't know to stand and offer a woman his seat.

Some people blame this on the entry of women into the work force, which necessitated changes in behavior. For example, it was once considered impolite for a man to offer to shake hands with a woman—he waited for her to proffer hers. Today the only gainfully employed lady to whom this rule

Remember when...
Failing to marry the mother of your child used to make you an outcast—instead of a fascinating public figure?

applies is Queen Elizabeth. When you meet her, wait. The trashiness epidemic, however, is not just reflected in etiquette; it is an attitude. Women, convinced that they were oppressed and prevented from reaching their full potential before the end of the 1950s, are often brittle and hostile towards men. If you want to see the way relations between the sexes have changed, two events, a hundred years apart, encapsulate the change.

When the *Costa Concordia* cruise liner struck rocks and rolled onto its side off the coast of Tuscany in 2012, passengers and the press alike compared the modern marine catastrophe to the sinking of the *Titanic* a hundred years earlier—a comparison that proved unflattering to the men of the *Costa Concordia*.

A century had wrought a sea change in the way the men aboard the ship behaved towards the female passengers. As an English newspaper headline queried in the wake of the *Costa Concordia* debacle:

"Whatever Happened to Women and Children First?"

What indeed? Men on the *Costa Concordia* elbowed their way past mothers, children, and pregnant women to claim the lifeboats and save their own sorry skins. A grandmother told the *Daily News*, "I was standing by the lifeboats and men, big men, were banging into me and knocking the girls."

By contrast, when it became clear that the *Titanic* was doomed, the captain issued the order: "Women and children first!" The men of the *Titanic*, with a few exceptions, were faithful to the order and the code it enshrined. Their chivalry can be read in the survival rates: 74 percent of the women were saved, while only 20 percent of the men survived. It is telling, as Rich Lowry observed in *National Review*, that more women from third class, located deep in the ship's bowels, survived than did men from first class.

One of the men who did survive was J. Bruce Ismay, chairman of the White Star Line, builder and operator of the *Titanic*. It is quite likely that many times over in the ensuing years the universally despised Ismay must have longed to be able to turn back the hands of the clock and not step into that lifeboat. Regarded as a coward, Ismay lived the rest

> *Remember when...*
> Getting a seat on a bus was more about "Women and children first" and less about "The strong do what they can, and the weak suffer what they must"?

of his life in disgrace. Respect for women, even if it required the ultimate sacrifice, was ingrained in the culture.

Forget giving up a seat in a lifeboat. For heaven's sake, today all too many able-bodied men won't give up so much as a seat on the bus. Whenever I see such an oaf sitting while ladies remain on their feet, I say to myself, "Well, I know what kind of mother *he* had." He may have had a mother like Lynn Messina, a novelist who wrote a piece for the *New York Times* entitled: "I Don't Want My Preschooler to be a 'Gentleman.'"

Something tells me that Mommie Rudest may succeed only too well. So, if you are the mother of daughters, take down her son's name and put him on the No Play Date list. Meanwhile, Ms. Messina explains why she doesn't want her little boy to become a gentleman:

> My 4-year-old son, Emmett, swallows a spoonful of cereal and asks me if I know what a gentleman is. Surprised, I tell him I have some idea; then I ask what the word means to him.
>
> "A gentleman lets girls go first," he says, explaining that every day at naptime all the girls go to the bathroom before the boys.
>
> His explanation, along with the quiet solemnity with which he delivers it, is completely endearing and yet it makes my heart ache. This adorable little boy, who is only beginning to learn the ways of the world, just got his first lesson in sexism—and from a teacher who, I don't doubt, believes she's doing something wonderful for womankind.

> Letting girls use the bathroom first isn't a show of respect. It is, rather, the first brick in the super high pedestal that allows men to exalt women out of sight....

The mothers of boys who grow up to be gentlemen spend a lot of time and energy building the pedestals that make it likely that their sons will treat women respectfully. Of course, it isn't the case that every man on the *Titanic* inwardly believed that every woman he helped into a lifeboat—thereby forfeiting his own life—was a superior being. But he knew that if he were to call himself a gentleman he had to respect women, even if he paid the ultimate price.

The alternative was becoming another Bruce Ismay. But I don't want it to appear as if this is a matter purely of dying in the name of etiquette and honor, as important as those things are. What really mattered was that the men of the *Titanic* didn't put themselves first. It is probably a little harder not to put yourself first when women regard you as a patriarchal oppressor, but ultimately not being trashy is not political: it's personal.

The decline in gentlemanly behavior has been blamed on many things—feminism, an urgent new sense of equality, or the project of modernity. Ms. Messina hides behind charges of "sexism." But why not call the boorish standards she seeks to instill in her son what they are: just plain White Trash?

White Trash Recipes–
for When You Want to Eat (and Drink) Like
Hit Don't Make No Difference

White Trash Desserts
Guilty Pleasures

"Honey, I'm a Ho" Cake

A culinary miracle inspired by the humble Ho Ho® Cake.

Ingredients:

- 1 box red velvet cake mix
- 3 eggs
- ⅓ cup vegetable oil
- 1¼ cups water
- 1 12-ounce box Hostess Twinkies® (can substitute Sara Lee® Golden Crème Cakes)
- 1 13-ounce box of Hostess Ho-Hos® (can substitute Little Debbie® Swiss Rolls)
- 2 1-ounce containers Betty Crocker® Cream Cheese Frosting
- Butter and flour for preparing pans

Preheat oven to 350°F. Butter two 9-inch cake pans. Cut two pieces of parchment paper to fit into the bottom of each pan. Place in pans, then butter tops of parchment paper. Sift a small amount of flour in each pan, turning so that the bottom and sides are coated. Turn upside down in the sink and tap out excess flour.

Place cake mix into a bowl or mixer with paddle attachment. Turn on low speed and add water, then eggs one at a time. Pour ½ cup of batter into each cake pan, spreading so the bottoms are covered. Arrange snack cakes in pans, alternating the varieties and leaving a small amount of room between the snack cakes. Pour remaining batter in pans and bake for 35 minutes, or until cake tops are firm. Let cool before removing from pans, then assemble and frost cake. Serves 12.

Hershey® Bar Pie

So delicious you won't be tempted to throw it in the event of a family argument.

Ingredients:
- 24 Oreo® cookies
- ¼ cup unsalted butter, melted
- 2 teaspoons cold butter for greasing pan
- ½ cup whole milk
- 20 marshmallows
- 6 Hershey® bars
- 8 ounces Cool Whip®

Preheat oven to 350°F. Grind Oreos® and melted butter in Cuisinart®; press into 9-inch pie pan to form a crust. Bake crust for 10 minutes; remove and let cool to room temperature. Heat milk and marshmallows on stovetop over medium heat, stirring constantly. Once marshmallows are melted, turn heat down to low and add Hershey® bars, stirring constantly until melted. Pour filling into piecrust and refrigerate or freeze for a minimum of 30 minutes. When ready to serve, remove and top with Cool Whip® topping. Serves 8.

Chapter Six

Bratz® and Brats

When you git right down to it, White Trash is sperled rotten.

While there are still some antediluvian souls who practice self-control and put themselves out to create a congenial atmosphere, White Trash traditionally has not been among them. The White Trash MO may be summed up thus: I'll do what I damned well please. If you don't like it, hit don't make noooo difference.

Come to think of it, doesn't that credo sound exactly like the bumptious modern child?

Here is a true story: The King family took their children—aged two, three, and eight—to an upscale Italian restaurant in Kingston, Washington, and upon receiving the bill, the parents noticed a $4 discount for "well-behaved kids." What gives? Not only had the miraculous King children said "please" and "thank you" but—gilding the lily—they had actually remained seated throughout the meal, as opposed to going from table to table, menacing other patrons with their cuteness.

It's a nice story. But there's a flip side. Not to take anything away from the polite King children, but this doesn't speak well for the rest of our Kadens, Kendras, and Kourtneys (we'll get to unfortunate White Trash naming patterns in a minute). The owner of the restaurant conceded as much. "So we go to the parents," he admitted, "and say 'I'm sorry but we really need little Johnny to sit down and not run around and yell and scream … because he's bothering some of the patrons.' And parents will take an attitude to the point where we're almost afraid to say something."

> ||||||||||||||||||||||||||||||||||||||||||||||||||||||||||||||||
>
> ## *Old White Trash*
> Underfed children behaving badly in Appalachia
>
> ## *New White Trash*
> Overfed children behaving badly in nice restaurants
>
> ||||||||||||||||||||||||||||||||||||||||||||||||||||||||||||||||

Some parents are embarrassed—to their credit. But still they are too supine to take a stand. So they find themselves paying for a fancy prep school and at the same time rearing a family of White Trash children. Judging from Internet etiquette sites, the question that haunts the modern parent is, "Can we take the kids to a nice restaurant?" The answer is yes, but only, only, only if the little darlings have had it drilled into their heads that they are to be seen and not heard—once a widely accepted maxim of childrearing.

When Oliver Wendell Holmes wrote *The Autocrat of the Breakfast Table*, he was not referring to an eleven-year-old. The child as the destroyer of civilized dining is a relatively new phenomenon. One of the nice bits in *Life with Father*, a collection of loosely autobiographical stories by Clarence Day Jr., published in 1936, comes when Father, Clarence Day Sr., a charmingly choleric New York stockbroker, takes the younger Clarence, still a little boy, who has come to visit his father's office on a Saturday morning, to lunch at Delmonico's, a fancy restaurant.

Father introduces Clarence Jr., who bobs politely, to the maître d'hôtel. After the formalities, Father proceeds to give himself totally to the delicious food. The son is seen but not heard, which doesn't prevent him from appreciating the fare and absorbing the ambience. Well, of course, not all of us can afford take the kids to Delmonico's. That's not the point. The point is that this was a father-centric rather than a child-centric dining experience. Father would have been appalled had young Clarence piped up with advice or sage political opinions. Caden, Cooper, and Caitlin, on the other hand, believe that they are the center of the universe and feel it is their duty to instruct Mummy and Daddy about the evils of plastic bags.

Unlike Clarence Day Jr., our children are pampered beyond words. We even play Beethoven for them when they are in the womb. As the radio host Lenore Skenazy has observed, this is taking unfair advantage of a captive audience.

Endless hovering, ironically, is not the best way to produce a disciplined, decent human being. "We love our children," Rachel Johnson, the English journalist, wrote,

> We want them to grow up to be competent, decent human beings fit for adult purpose. But not only does our coddling of the young fail to prepare them for leaving the nest, the rigours of employment, self-catering, London transport and earning a living in a recession, it doesn't even prepare them to do the most basic of household tasks. Having members of society who have only ever been feather-bedded, pampered, chauffeured from A to B, privately tutored, and had their bottoms wiped since birth is bad news for us all. We have bred a generation of spoilt, rude incompetents.

A friend of mine who is otherwise quite modern in her outlook raised two delightful sons, now attractive young men, by the simple expedient of threatening to send them to bed without dessert whenever they got the least bit out of line at the dinner table. Okay, I'm oversimplifying. There were other childrearing techniques involved. But the threat, which, by the way, was not idle, was magic. Moreover, it presupposed two conditions not inevitably present nowadays:

Remember when...
Teenagers used to aspire to be adults—instead of the other way around?

1) family dinner, and 2) that parents, not children, ruled the roost. In other words, the parents civilized their offspring, while at the same time they were able to enjoy their meal.

When children behave as if they were brought up in a barn—a favorite expression, by the way, of my mother—it is almost always the fault of indulgent adults. Whenever I did something awful, Mama would say, "Were you brought up in a barn?" I was often tempted to say, "Yes, Ma'am." My mother's step-grandmother (I told you we were a were a crazy, intergenerational Southern family under one roof with more loose screws than the Nelsons) was fond of saying, "When children turn twelve, they become very silly and you must send them away until they get over it." (This is admittedly not feasible for many families today. They are, after all, stuck with nursery school bills that amount to more than the cost of my college education. They may also erroneously believe that boarding school is cruel.)

Old White Trash
Not enough social polish

New White Trash
Too much sense of entitlement

One of my least favorite ads is one for a bank, featuring a gaggle of tots sitting around a table with a lone adult, who asks them their opinion on whether it's better to do one or two things at a time. The question really sets the kids off. They gyrate and wiggle and agree that it's better to duo-task. But really, do we care what children think? Okay, it's just an advertisement. But there are people who actually *care what children think*. The wisdom of Mama's step-grandmother is neglected all too often today. But the truth remains. Children are silly, and indeed, are supposed to be silly—it's part of being a child. Adults are making a horrible miscalculation if they don't recognize this and act accordingly. Repeat after me: not everything Caden says is oracular, cute, or even mildly amusing. White Trash families might have found it a hoot and a half when Baby Jethro expressed hisself by gleefully flinging around scraps of possum meat at chow time. But in better times nice parents worked overtime to repress their children at every turn. That was what made them nice. Wallowing (another favorite word of my mother's, used when anybody dared to sit on a bed during daylight) in self-expression was discouraged. Here is a sentence that you would not have heard in the halcyon days before White Trash

> *Remember when...*
> Children had dolls and fire trucks—instead of political opinions?

Normal: "I voted for President Obama because Caden absolutely insisted."

Caden is twelve.

That reminds me of the time I realized to my horror that the world was coming to an end because of overpopulation. I was in junior high school, and I rushed home to impart this disturbing news. How my family laughed and laughed! Hard as it may be for the modern family to believe, my family was serenely unconcerned with what I thought about the population bomb. It was not quite yet a child-centric era. The essence of trashiness is behaving as if the world revolves around you; being civilized is making other people feel welcome and valued. This applies particularly to children, as there are few things on earth more appalling than a little person with a sense of entitlement and self-righteous opinions about global warming. This truth was once universally acknowledged even in the highest circles—especially in the highest circles.

For example, when Queen Elizabeth II was a child, she was on some occasion rude to one of her mother's ladies-in-waiting. Instead of allowing the royal toddler to pull rank, her mother, then queen, took corrective action, admonishing the future monarch that she was a princess who must endeavor to become "a lady." Moral of the story: even if the world does revolve around you, it is trashy to act like it. Princess Elizabeth, who has led a life of duty, was taught this lesson early on, but our Cadens and Bradens absorb a

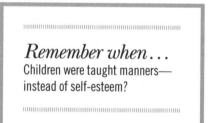

Remember when...
Children were taught manners—instead of self-esteem?

different lesson. Everything in their little lives is designed to enhance their self-esteem. So how's that working out?

Modern children, pampered and pushed and made all too aware of status—a vulgar subject—before they have left the care of Nanny (herself, alas, all too often treated as only a living, breathing status symbol by pushy parents), have a high notion of their own importance. Respect for adults, even poor adults (indeed, especially poor ones), once the defining characteristic of nice children, is less common now. When I was Honey Boo Boo's age, the worst thing that could be said of a child was, "She is rude to grownups." I still have a chilling recollection of being told by my playmate Jennifer Williams that I was rude to adults. It was all I could do not to run her down with my tricycle. The memory haunts me yet. One of my pet peeves is little children who don't say "ma'am" and "sir" to adults. Some people consider this archaic, but the children of all my Southern friends do it. I'll never forget the day the child of a friend caught a fish in Deer Creek and dragged it around all day on a string. The fish was dead and smelly. No self-respecting cat would have deigned to touch it. "Throw the fish back," Mummy ordered liltingly, when she realized what was going on. "We don't want to be cruel to animals, do we?" she said sweetly. "No, Ma'am," said the fish-killing kinder sweetly. (Of course one does not say ma'am, by the way, as I am sure we all recall, to a younger person; after a certain stage in life, one is more ma'amed against than ma'aming.) Children must also have it drummed into their heads that they must spring to their feet whenever an adult— any adult—enters the room. Otherwise, they will get above themselves.

Some misguided people prefer that even children they are just meeting address them by their first names. Being called Mrs. or Mr. makes them feel old. Miss Manners has noted perceptively that being called by your first name doesn't make you any younger. I am stunned when strangers of any age use my first name without even asking. Still, I love being called Charlotte by my friends' children, and some children of especially old friends even call me Chee, as I am sometimes known below the Mason-Dixon Line. But the tone is set by us oldies, not the children. Even as a child I called my godmother's parents Bess and Dunbar—but it was my mother, not I, who decided that Bess and Dunbar might like this. Uncontrollable children were still an anomaly.

While on one hand children are catered to today, they are also exposed to a blunt coarseness that previous generations were protected from. When it comes to picking up graphic details about the human anatomy, growing up in a one-room shack in Skunk Hollow has nothing on a stroll through the toy department of a department store. Once upon a time, dolls didn't look like hookers. "Stripper" was not the first word that leapt to mind when you saw Terri Lee®, a dolly popular with us Baby Boomers. Like most of the little girls who played with her, Terri Lee® had a Brownie® uniform in her wardrobe. She was never going to be run in on a morals charge.

Cloe, Jade, Sasha, Meygan, and Roxxi— the sexpot Bratz® dolls— are an altogether different kettle of fishnet hose. Sold at such outlets as Walmart®, Target®, and Toys "R" Us®, the strangely shaped Bratz® dolls wear tons of eye shadow. Their outfits

Old White Trash
Teenaged girls with dirty fingernails

New White Trash
Teenaged girls with breast implants

would never do for Sunday school. Not to put too fine a point on it, Slutz might be a better moniker for the line. "They look like pole dancers on their way to work at a gentlemen's club," Margaret Talbot wrote. "You could never imagine a Bratz doll assuming any of the dozens of careers Barbie has pursued over the decades: not Business Executive or Surgeon or Summit Diplomat—not even Pan Am Flight Attendant or Pet Doctor." But there is some good news: if you check out the Bratz® dolls' online bios, they all appear to be vegetarians. No doubt that's to set a good example for the children. But no one seems concerned about what else they may be learning from these edgy toys—or from increasingly sexualized children's entertainment. One of my friends speaks glumly of the "skanky fairies" on a popular children's show. "One of them looks like Tinker Bell in go-go boots," she says ruefully, adding—hopelessly—"and she's the nice one." Oh, dear—slutz fairies.

Just one more observation before we leave the Bratz® girls: those names. The Bratz® may have exaggerated bodies, but those names are pretty much what you're going to get in a normal kindergarten class today. It's unfortunate, too, since a nice name is absolutely free. Roxxi and Cloe are not nice names. Megan is a nice name, but unless you have a Great-Aunt Meygan—which is highly improbable—Meygan is puredee trash. Ditto Jade. Well, it's fine if White Trash parents and developers of risqué toys for children want to pluck names out of thin air, but now everybody does it. "I like the name Cooper," an intern said, when she was talking of having children one day. "Are there a lot of Coopers in your family?" I asked innocently. Nope, it was just a name she liked, and she was going to use it, White Trash fashion. I feel it highly likely that Cooper will have a sister named Madison.

One of the disheartening developments is the invention of new names by the destruction of old names: Aidan was a saint. Kaden and Caden are made-up names. I'm told that there is a variation on this name for every letter in the alphabet. I shudder.

I take a pro-family name position despite my unfortunate middle name: Everett. Yes, my middle name is Everett, which I've always thought sort of tacky, but it paid for my education. When I was born, my grandfather came to the

Old White Trash
Naming your daughter Daisy Mae

New White Trash
Naming your daughter Daizi

hospital and whispered to Mama, "Stick an Everett in there." It turned out to be a fortuitous suggestion, as my parents were not great planners. The college money came in handy. It was a middle name of several four-named men in my family, one of whom came through with the cash. In time I came to appreciate my name. Besides, while it may be tacky to be an Everett, it's a whole lot tackier to default on a guvmint student loan. No, I'm not saying that every great-uncle with an unfortunate middle name is going to pay your college tuition. But I am saying it is nice to be connected with your own roots, and nothing does that like a name.

A possible reason for the White Trashing of family names is a resentful attitude towards history. For genuinely poor people, there may have been a sense, right or wrong, that history had dealt them a bad hand. More affluent parents must pay fancy prep schools to teach their children that American history sucks, but even public school kids can acquire a sense of grievance. When I was in high school, we used to chant a little ditty. "Latin is a dead language," we'd sing, "as dead as it can be. It killed the ancient Romans, and now it's killing me." Unfortunately, they finally got to Latin, which is as dead as dead can be for most high school kids today. Instead of Latin or history, children learn about personal development. The result is getting stuck in the present and not caring about one's origins. We used to associate ignorance with the underclass. Not any more.

Feminists, who are often so hostile to the past, should take a more traditional line on names. Middle names, after all, were once generally a mother's or grandmother's maiden name. Until recently, you could chart the saga of your family through the names. I love knowing about the Charlotte for whom I am specifically named and about all the other Charlottes, and how the name came into the family. It amazes me that Charlotte—a Goldilocks name, being not too plain and also not too fancy—has fallen out of fashion. I complained about this to my sister, Julia. "I guess I have to get rich or win a Pulitzer Prize to get a namesake," I huffed. "Maybe you should try for a Pulitzer," she not very helpfully suggested. Please buy my book: I am trying to save up the money to bribe one of my great-nieces to name somebody Charlotte.

White Trash Recipes–
for When You Want to Eat (and Drink) Like
Hit Don't Make No Difference

White Trash Sandwiches
Appealing to the Classic White Trash Vices—Gluttony and Sloth

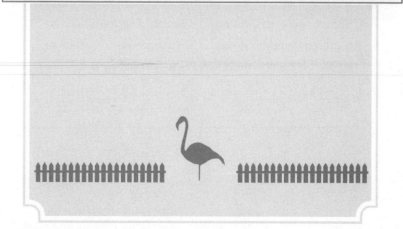

Elvis Special

Elvis, an early exemplar of White Trash Normal, was partial to a version of this peanut-butter-and-banana sandwich. (No wonder he was on diet pills.)

Ingredients:
- 1 banana
- 2 tablespoons peanut butter
- 2 slices Wonder Bread®
- 3 tablespoons butter

Mash banana in a bowl with a fork. Spread peanut butter over one piece of bread. Heat one tablespoon butter in a skillet over medium heat. Sauté banana in butter; remove from pan and place on top of peanut butter, then finish sandwich with second piece of bread. Add another tablespoon of butter to skillet, then place sandwich in pan. Cook until lightly browned, then flip over. Add remaining butter to pan and cook until browned. Remove, slice in half, and serve immediately. Serves 1.

Mayonnaise Sandwich

The ultimate White Trash snack.

Ingredients:
- 2 slices Wonder Bread®
- 3 tablespoons Miracle Whip®

Gently spread Miracle Whip® on bread. Serves 1.

Chapter Seven

A Fork in the Road

As I sit across the table in a fancy restaurant from an Ivy League graduate watching him snarf down bouillabaisse, I marvel: Didn't his mother think to mention that dinner partners should not be obliged to avert their eyes to avoid a view of one's tonsils? As Conrad's Mister Kurtz observed in a different context: "The Horror! The Horror!"

We were at an informal luncheon in a hotel ballroom. I was idly musing that the guest to my left, a well-known policy wonk, was wearing an extremely expensive suit but had just stabbed her meat as if she expected it to get up and run away. It was at this precise moment that her hand darted forward, plucked a toothpick from the pork roll, and proceeded to apply the implement liberally to her front teeth. Like any self-respecting Southerner, I blamed her mother. I do the same when I see oafs sitting on the bus while elderly ladies stand.

We are at a fork in the road. We regularly deplore bad manners and sense how much more pleasant our daily existence might be if people observed a few basics—chew with your mouth closed, don't use vulgar language on the bus, stand up for a lady, and don't address somebody you are just meeting by his first name unless you are asked to do so. Etiquette, unlike Gaul, is divided into two parts: the formal rules of etiquette and the informal rules of simple decency. Both enhance our lives. Both are under attack. If crudity wins, I have but one request: shoot me. Please.

> *Old White Trash*
> The Snopeses
>
> *New White Trash*
> The Kardashians

But this isn't just a chapter about how to hold your fork. Our plight is much worse than anything Emily Post ever dreamed of. I recently saw a show on TLC about parsons' wives that featured the parson showing his daughters how to put condoms on bananas. An installment of Bravo's *Pregnant in Heels* had host Rosie Pope demonstrating what she called "fart spray," available in her Los Angeles shop. "How does that not draw attention to the fact that you are just farting everywhere?" an assistant asks.

Old-line White Trash didn't know a lot about the formal rules of proper etiquette, but I can't help thinking they were a bit more genial than New White Trash; they respected age and had a sense of boundaries (between the Hatfields and McCoys, for instance). New White Trash, by contrast, is often condescending and endowed with a thoroughly undeserved sense of privilege. Occasionally, I have to give an assignment to a younger co-worker—who inevitably expects me to have already done the work. Do I have all the phone numbers they'll need? Can I send them the research? No and no. Old White Trash was bumptious; New White Trash is boorish.

But like Old White Trash, New White Trash are sloppy and untutored with regard to the rules, formal and informal. Unlike Old White Trash, however, they rarely feel ill-at-ease about this lack. They may have an obligation to eat locally, but they rarely feel compelled to make life easier for those who are serving them their organic goodies. *Noblesse oblige* (another quaint term) went out the window long ago. It was certainly not *noblesse oblige* that obliged former Speaker of the House Nancy Pelosi to demand repeatedly

Remember when…
Common courtesy actually was common?

that, whenever Madame Speaker had to return to her district in California, the military drop everything and provide her with a private plane, well-stocked with munchies, alcohol, and bottled water, to ferry her and various members of her family across this great nation. Privilege coupled with bad manners makes New White Trash a plague on civilization.

One of the most annoying things about being alive today is that total strangers use our first names without asking. This is abrasive and makes life just a bit less pleasant. When my sister was responsible for an elderly relative many years ago, she was horrified that the nurses kept addressing their charge as "Ginny." Ginny this, Ginny that. "Ginny," it seems, was adamant about not taking a morsel of sustenance.

Until her confinement in the nursing home, nobody had ever called the patient (whose given name was Virginia) Ginny in all her life—much less spoken to her in a tone of singsong condescension. She was, moreover, of such an advanced age that she probably hadn't even been called Virginia for many years. "I think you might have more luck," my sister ventured, "if you call her Mrs. Jones."

It worked like a charm. Though ailing and seemingly unable to comprehend what was going on around her, the old lady immediately relaxed her guard and began eating her supper. A little respect, which includes a dollop of distance, goes a long way. Older people, once regarded as venerable, are now victims of familiarity, treated as if they are children.

Maybe I am antediluvian, but I hate to be called by my first name by strangers. It rubs me the wrong way. Even more, I hate to see any older man or woman disrespected in this way. Not too long ago, waiting to see the dermatologist, I witnessed the unedifying spectacle of an elderly patient shambling to the receptionist's desk after being summoned with the words, "Nick! I need your insurance card."

Soon it was my turn for the assault on my dignity. When beckoned sans honorific by a young woman who obviously had patterned her demeanor on Pauline, the slatternly receptionist on *Doc Martin*, it was all I could do to keep from saying, "Since we have only just met, my dear, I am going to ask you to call me by a special little name I reserve for my new friends—Miss Hays." (No, I didn't say it, and I know that if I had the Pauline reenactor would have called me by a special little name that rhymes with rich.)

Instead of giving an impromptu etiquette lesson—always tempting but, alas, to be avoided, as it is rude and will likely fall on deaf ears anyway—I simply found a new doctor. My new dermatologist's receptionists are polite young women who are friendly but not overly familiar. And I made a discovery: the physician whose receptionists are polite is also the one who listens more attentively to his patients.

When it comes to dealing with computer people or telemarketers, I inevitably feel like Alex Haley's character Kunta Kinte. Kunta Kinte's slave name was Toby, and so he had to go around constantly saying that his name was Kunta Kinte. My name is Miss Hays, or in a pinch, Ms. Hays, if I have not previously had the pleasure of making your acquaintance. But I hate, hate, hate to ask people to call me Miss Hays, especially the computer folks or telemarketers, who, truth to tell, have signed on for one of society's most unpleasant jobs. Indeed, there used to be a rule, no doubt now long forgotten, that one never signed a letter with a title. Even the Queen of England signs Elizabeth R (though that R is a dead giveaway that she is somebody important).

So, no, I don't like asking to be called Miss Hays. But I've gotten so I do it. For one thing, since I am enormously ignorant about computers (a friend accuses me of sending many Indian youths to forsake their jobs in tech support to go and live in the slums rather than deal with me), the call is likely to be lengthy ("What is a portal?"). I want both of us to be as comfortable as possible. By the way, I call the person on the other end Mr. or Ms. Many computer technical people are scrupulously polite and would eschew familiarity if their bosses didn't write these hideous scripts for them.

Telemarketers tend to be more annoying. Always remember when you are tempted to be rude to them: they have chosen to work at a job many Americans would seek government help rather than do. That the firms which produce these scripts believe we want to get chummy over a subscription renewal doesn't bode well for civilization. More offensive are the canned calls that inevitably follow. I don't mind a *soupçon* of insincerity, but I refuse to take it from a machine.

Perhaps it was pure coincidence that the better doctor had the more polite receptionist. But I don't think so. While courtesy signals competence, rudeness just as often is a signal of the opposite. John Humphrys, the BBC broadcaster, noticed the same thing when he was assigned to report on schools in the UK. "I spent a year making a BBC Two documentary about the state of education in Britain," Humphrys recalled in the *Daily Telegraph*,

> and if I took away one single incontestable fact it was that the schools where the teachers were respected were the schools that delivered the best education. And 'respect' meant the children did not swear in their presence. Ever. National treasure with a brain the size of Jupiter Mr. [Stephen] Fry may be [on record as saying using bad language is

a really important part of life and people who can't
see that are 'mad, silly and prissy'], but I'd love to
have heard him explaining his barmy ideas to those
teachers.

Southern mothers, still bucking the trash talk trend, work
overtime to make sure that their progeny will reflect well on
them. Southern belles may be terribly self-centered, but with
help from their mothers they learn to hide it, especially with
regard to being kind to older people, whom they still address,
unless requested to do otherwise, as ma'am or sir rather than
Nick or Ginny. "Manners are a sensitive awareness of the
feelings of others. If you have that awareness, you have good
manners, no matter which fork you use," Emily Post said.
How very true, although I feel certain Miss Post cared
intensely about using the right fork. The Victorians invented
a vast array of pieces of silver (fish knives and fish forks are
Victorian and unnecessary) to test people. It is not necessary
to go that far. I do not believe that in this day and age you
need to know how to use the marrow scoop. But familiarity
with the basics and knowing how to set the table correctly
show a certain respect for order, one's dinner partners, and
those who have gone before us.

Self-respecting Southern mothers make it a point never to
let their children take a bite of food in peace. Nice Southern
mothers never allow the opportunity for a small etiquette
lesson to pass unutilized. Southern children are always being
told things such as, when soup is to be eaten, "little boats go
out to sea." Sometimes I think it has made us Southerners
suffer unnecessarily, but not in the way you might think: I die

a thousand deaths when somebody who should have known better leaves a spoon in a soup bowl and avert my eyes when I see the ukulele grasp—holding the knife almost straight up and making use of four fingers rather than just the index finger to guide it, an increasingly widespread habit.

Speaking of proper dining etiquette, hailing from a class that isn't even recognized any more—Shabby Genteel—I have a proper horror of picking up the wrong fork. The Shabby Genteel is the class George Orwell, a member of the SG UK branch, described as people who have nothing to lose but their aitches. In other words, to make up for not being filthy rich, we put a lot of emphasis on intangibles. Maybe some of our small snobberies were silly (my mother remembered until her dying day that a cousin of mine had used blue ink to answer a formal invitation). But would it really be such a bad thing if children were instructed in how to answer a formal invitation properly? Or perhaps instructed just to answer an invitation! Is it such a bad idea to know how to tackle a larger-than-usual array of forks? (My friend Craig Shackelford says this can be boiled down to a few simple rules: big plate, big fork, small plate, small fork, and go from the outside in.)

> *Remember when...*
> Being scruffy and rude didn't make you cool or "authentic"?

Shabby Genteel born and bred, I must admit that the fork question loomed quite large in my childhood. What, I wondered, would you do if you went somewhere and there was an unfamiliar fork? The rule was to watch the hostess, which I regard as a model of paying attention to others. Etiquette, like harmless gossip, is the ultimate expression of interest in others. My Watch Others rule was put to the test when I went to a fancy dinner in the apartment of a prominent New York hostess. I sat between a famous dress designer and an intimate of Mrs. Reagan's known for his rudeness. I was terrified. There were finger bowls. It took a few minutes, but I realized to my horror that I wasn't the only person present who had no idea what to do. Do you move them to the side or do you dip your fingers? I still can't remember what we did, but whatever we did, we did it without fanfare. It is not necessary to know how to use a finger bowl, by the way. It is necessary to know how to handle yourself when confronted with something unfamiliar.

For the record, unkindness worries me more than the wrong fork ever could. The worst incident of unkindness I've ever seen when dining out—still remembered after all these years—took place in a New Orleans restaurant when I was in my twenties. I was dining with a band of fellow socialists (yes, we all have our checkered pasts). The commies didn't much like some dish or other and insisted the poor cook come from the kitchen to explain what had gone wrong. He was a wretched older man, cowering in the face of blistering criticism from young jerks. So much for solidarity with the people.

Like my commie friends, many people today expect to be catered to and are incredibly spoiled. Whenever I see a motorcade in Washington, D.C., I wonder what minor official has decided he is too important to drive himself. This doesn't, of course, apply to the First Family—any First Family—who should be accorded high honors, although it would be appreciated if they behaved a bit more like the King and Queen of England during the blitz, when the royals observed some of the same rationing rules as applied to regular folks. Luxury is no substitute for propriety.

You know those jerks who speak loudly on their cell phones on the bus or train? Miss Post would have hoped they might become more aware of the presence of others, who might not be so interested in their mergers, both professional and personal. We become a captive audience for some boor who doesn't seem to care

> *Remember when...*
> Taking public transportation meant small talk with the other passengers—rather than being held a captive audience to their private conversations?

that private details are not for public consumption and may, in fact, be quite boring. A study published in the journal *Plos One* found that much of the annoyance caused by overheard cell phone conversations comes from a "blurring of the distinction between the public and the private sphere." But cell phones are a mere vehicle. We have become a society that airs our dirty linen in public, whether on a freaky "reality" television show or via cell phone. In the case of cell phones, the study found, members of the captive audience were angry at having no control over the situation.

People who use cell phones to make long personal calls in public places are pioneers of rudeness, enlisting technological advances to make life not more but less agreeable to all of us.

Cell phones are used to ignore those actually present. The woman at the corner grocery mart never interrupts her cell phone conversations to ring up my purchases. I've been shopping there for years, yet I am not real to her. I can understand why taxi drivers might need to phone home occasionally. But lengthy discussions in a foreign language are rude. Sorry, multiculturalists, but they are. On long rides to the airport, say, I combat this annoyance by singing hymns at the top of my lungs: whenever the driver is on the phone, I sing a song of the saints of God or belt forth, "Jerusalem!" Arguably, I am being rude. Still, as I can't carry a tune, this ploy more often than not works.

While annoying people regale us with too much information, we are less likely to see the once-common polite exchanges that created public civility. We are too engrossed in ourselves to make eye contact when speaking to somebody helping us in the supermarket, to say thank you, or to wish the bus driver a nice day. We no longer make polite conversation with strangers about the weather, an expression not of interest in the weather but of (mild) interest in another human being. While such small courtesies are on the wane, personal revelation is waxing. A college professor friend of mine tells about the coed who couldn't make it to class. Instead of sending a brief email saying merely that she was sick, she launched into a lengthy description of the gory details of the problems she was having with her birth control pills.

We live in a gilded age that is also a very rude age. We neglect manners in part because we don't care. A second reason for our rudeness is even more damning: many people, especially some highly vocal ones, are hostile to the whole

Revenge on the Cell Phone Boor

The final word on cell phone rudeness belongs, as in the case of swear words, to the aforementioned John Humphrys, the BBC broadcaster who contributed a chapter to *How Rude!: Modern Manners Defined*, published by Waitrose, the UK grocery chain. (Safeway, Giant, are you listening? Or such a project might be a particularly appropriate undertaking for Harris Teeter, the Southern grocery chain.) When a woman on a train provided her fellow passengers with more than they cared to know about her life, according to Humphrys, one of the trapped passengers managed to send her a text message. It said something like: "As a result of being forced to listen to your conversation for the past two hours I now know a great deal about your private and professional life, including your name, phone number and credit card details. I have noted them down and rest assured I shall make good use of them if you do not shut up immediately." The woman went berserk, running up and down the aisle, demanding to know who had texted her. Nobody fessed up and nobody squealed. Several urged her to pipe down.

While one should generally refrain from reprimanding others in public, there may be instances such as this when it simply must be done.

concept of traditional manners. Formality and indeed simple decency are holdovers from a class-based past. Remember, we're all supposed to hate each other now. In an article in the *New Republic* that managed to be both breathtakingly snobbish and stupidly against common courtesy at the same time, Tim Noah took on the scourge of businesses that— gasp!—have the audacity to require that their employees be pleasant to the public.

Noah wrote,

> Pret A Manger—a London-based chain that has
> spread over the past decade to the East Coast and
> Chicago—is at the cutting edge of what the
> Berkeley sociologist Arlie Hochschild calls
> "emotional labor." Emotional because the worker
> doesn't create or even necessarily sell a product or
> service so much as make the customer experience
> a positive feeling....
>
> Fast-food service is not one of the caring
> professions. The only imperatives typically
> addressed in a Pret shop are hunger and thirst. Why
> must the person who sells me a cheddar and tomato
> sandwich have "presence" and "create a sense of
> fun"? Why can't he or she be doing it "just for the
> money"? I don't expect the swiping of my credit
> card to be anybody's vocation. This is, after all, the
> economy's bottommost rung.

I know Tim, and I can vouch that he is a very nice person. However, that line about the Pret A Manger employees being "the economy's bottommost rung" takes my breath away. Really, it does. Does Tim actually believe that the well-groomed folks at Pret A Manger are as low as you can go? And even if they were, so what? Would that absolve them of the obligation to be cordial to the customers whose patronage pays their salaries?

Pret A Manger employees, by the way, apparently don't share Tim's view of them as the dregs of society. The *New*

York Times reported that turnover at the sandwich shops is lower than the fast food industry average—60 percent as compared to a rate that is normally 300 to 400 percent. As much as I abhor the term "caring profession," I greatly prefer somebody who pretends to care rather than ignoring me by talking on the cell phone. By the way, I owe the server the same courtesy. Together, we can make my bacon and avocado sandwich a good experience for both of us.

Like me, writer Sonny Bunch of the *Washington Free Beacon* doesn't see the employees at Pret A Manger as downtrodden escapees from a Hogarth etching. Bunch had an intriguing take on Tim's clarion call for rudeness. "What Noah seems most perturbed by is not that customer service is on the upswing," Bunch wrote. "Rather, he wants the predatory bourgeois class to see those who toil on the economy's 'bottommost rung' in their natural state: sorrow-filled and snarling, cursing their lowly lot in life. He might not necessarily want the worker to feel bad—but he certainly wants the *customer* to feel bad for the worker."

Tim Noah espouses a class warfare view of manners. If you are jostled in the street, it is because you belong to the oppressor class. Foul language on the subway? You've got it coming. Picking up the proper fork? My dear, use it to stab a member of the bourgeois class. It is *right* to shove people and use the F-word because you have been oppressed. Once, when I was elbowed by a man crossing the street, the ugly truth dawned on me: this guy has been told he has a *right* to hit me in the ribs. A second ugly thought dawned on me: I bet he'd be afraid to do this to a big strong man. Thuggish behavior is not only acceptable but commendable according to the Tim

Noah Guide to Perfect Etiquette. I daresay Tim and his intellectually trendy buddies don't behave so rudely, but it is a fact that our charmless educated elite have pretty sharp elbows.

We saw uncouthness elevated to new heights by the elite during the mercifully short life of the Occupy Wall Street movement. In Washington, D.C., Occupy thugs shoved an elderly woman to the ground, while in a San Diego Walmart occupiers filled seventy-five carts with merchandise and then fled, leaving the clean-up to the employees, who had chosen to do an honest day's work instead of having fun defecating on police cars or beating drums into the wee hours in a residential neighborhood.

Arnold Toynbee, our cicerone through our hellish tour of White Trash Normal, theorized, as has been noted already, that societies in decay reach into the underclass (a term not yet in vogue in Toynbee's day) for their manners and morals because the once-dominant "creative minority" has lost its luster. Our once-dominant "creative minority" hasn't just lost its luster. Its members have been turned into hate objects. We are taught that the people who built this country or those who have subsequently become rich or at least affluent in more recent times have somehow stolen from the rest of us. The very term "give back," which is what rich people are now expected to call it when they donate to charity, implies that they have stolen something. ("Property is theft" is a thoroughly White Trash sentiment.) It is thus no wonder that we reject formalities and niceties viewed as an inheritance from a disgraceful past during which a genocidal elite blazed its way from sea to shining sea by killing or enslaving everybody in its path. Caveat: making lots of money in the entertainment industry or from some other socially acceptable line of work is fine.

Manners aren't only skin-deep, they come from somewhere, and much of our crudeness comes from a rejection of our noble past. Yes, it was a noble past, and only if we regain an appreciation for it will be cease to be crude and rude and—yes—ill-educated. Project Appreciation should be doable since much of what we are told about our past is rooted in fantasy and ideology. You have no doubt heard that the original Europeans who came to these shores were "illegal aliens" who committed genocide against the nice Indians who forgot to check their papers. There are many ways of looking at history, and the founding is not my subject, but this is a way of looking at the past through the lens of a small modern clique of ideologues. If you read a bit of colonial history without blinders on, however, you will learn that the colonists originally saw the Indians as potential converts to Christianity (which, of course, our academic elites are likely to see as worse than genocide!).

Our early history is complex, and we should not underplay the brutality on either side. But we should do some reading before we docilely accept the trendy notion that our predecessors were genocidal maniacs. Nor should we forget the courage of the men and women who came to the wilderness and began the process of building a great country. Should the colonists have remained at home in Europe? Native Americans came from somewhere else, too. People move—it's happened throughout recorded history and long before we began to write history. Slavery was common throughout history, and we should be proud that our country spilt blood, and plenty of it, to end the institution on our shores.

Many people today are credentialed but not educated. We used to speak of certain people as being "beautifully educated," a description that implied finesse with a foreign language, good manners, and good grammar. If you were to quote today the marvelous motto of one venerable Oxford College, supplied by fourteenth-century bishop William of Wykeham, that "Manners maketh man," you'd get a blistering lecture from a feminist. Men who might otherwise quite like to open the door for a female of the species are often afraid to do so. We do have to make etiquette adjustments to accommodate women in the workplace, but was it really necessary to tear down the whole of human civilization? Please, if you see Miss Hays struggling with a heavy old door, don't hesitate to open it! (I am also fond of coats thrown over puddles à la Sir Walter Raleigh, but that might be too much to ask.)

Manners and character are entwined. Dick Meyer reflected on William of Wykeham's aphorism in a book entitled *Why We Hate Us: American Discontent in the New Millennium*. "In today's world that motto makes about as much sense as 'The world is flat,'" Meyer wrote. "If manners maketh man, man today is unmade." Civic virtue and manners were what Alexis de Tocqueville had in mind when he wrote about "habits of the heart." Meyer wrote in particular of a phenomenon that has been called emotional incontinence. Think of the college student who wrote at length to her professor about her problems with her birth control pills.

The New A.D. (After Diana)— the Dawn of White Trash Normal

If you want to date the coming of the Age of Airing Dirty Linen in Public, which is another way to say emotional incontinence, you might put it at the death of Princess Diana of Wales in 1997. We were crying in public and sloppily revealing far more to total strangers than they wanted to know about us long before Diana died in a drunk driving accident, but the outpouring of emotions without restraint at the time of her death was something new. The emotional orgy was occasioned by something more than the intrinsic sadness of the situation, great though that was. Diana, aiming to weaken if not to outright topple the monarchy, had promoted a cult of spilling the beans. "She had shared her feelings and weaknesses. Her upper lip was not always stiff, though always glossed," Meyer wrote. Princess Diana was more than a mere princess—she lives on as the patron saint of every grandmother who has ever slept with her daughter's husband and lived to tell about it on reality TV.

We are all Snopeses, the White Trash family in Faulkner, now. You don't have to go on TV and reveal your deviant behavior or tune in on a weekly basis to *Here Comes Honey Boo Boo* to be White Trash. All it takes is being sloppy, self-absorbed, and inconsiderate. And a dash of belligerence won't come amiss. The prevalence of White Trash manners has made riding on the subway all too often an X-rated experience, with vulgar words and amorous couples who take time out from kissing only for a fleeting moment to give you a hostile look lest you complain.

Although etiquette is properly something taught at the hearth, the proliferation of etiquette classes is a sign that we may have had enough of the abrasiveness of White Trash Normal in manners. Matt Ritchel reported in the *New York Times* last year that some expensive restaurants are setting aside family dining evenings that become etiquette tutorials. Other parents are signing up for classes for children that can cost anywhere from $300 to $1,200.

What is unfortunate is that many parents, still at least partly in the grip of White Trash Normal, are afraid to or don't know how to teach their children how to behave. "Some of these manners-minders acknowledge that they can sound like curmudgeons, just another generation of older folks mourning the lost habits of more refined times," the *Times* reported. "But they also say that parents welcome their efforts as a way of outsourcing the hard work of teaching youngsters to follow rules." Not perfect, but better than letting your child go through life thinking that using a toothpick is A-OK if you are wearing Armani.

Manners are more than something we see on the surface. They encompass the whole person. Unless we embrace the small inconveniences that being considerate includes (as compared to the enormous inconveniences wrought by the absence of manners), we will limp along as neo–White Trash. I leave you with a story. One night I stayed at a bed and breakfast in Petersburg, Virginia, the town where my grandfather grew up. My lodgings put me in mind of the Bates Motel, but that's a tale for another time. I had come not to see the famous battlefield but because I was going to a lunch with a relative. I went walking bright and early the next morning (*not* having been murdered in my bed by the heavily made-up gentleman who ran the guest house) and saw what appeared to be a tombstone in a front yard.

Who, I wondered, had been buried in the front yard on Sycamore Street? Weird. I crossed the street and looked more closely. It was then that I realized that I was standing in a place I'd heard about all my life. The monument wasn't a gravestone, but a marker for the spot on which a school established by Captain William Gordon McCabe, artillerist turned schoolmaster, had once stood. McCabe was my grandfather's beloved schoolteacher. And there, bringing a tear to my eye, was McCabe's famous motto:

> *"You may not all be scholars, but you can all be gentlemen."*

Have you ever heard such an anti-White Trash sentiment? That's heresy today. But it spoke to the notion of the whole person, the gentleman (and, by extension, the lady), who, if he can, masters the difficult academic subjects—but, more important, cultivates character. That character was expressed in manners. If we are ever to slay the beast of White Trash Normal, we must regain the sensibility that says that being a gentleman, or a lady, is the most important thing we can achieve. And here's the really good news: that's something anybody can do.

A White Trash Timeline

Some Milestones on the Road to White Trash Normal

1936

The first Tampax® ad is published in a national magazine, setting off a wave of increasingly frank advertising for previously unmentionable feminine hygiene products. Without this pioneering moment, civilization might have missed out on Viagra's® ubiquitous four-hour-erection commercial and Bob Dole's erectile dysfunction.

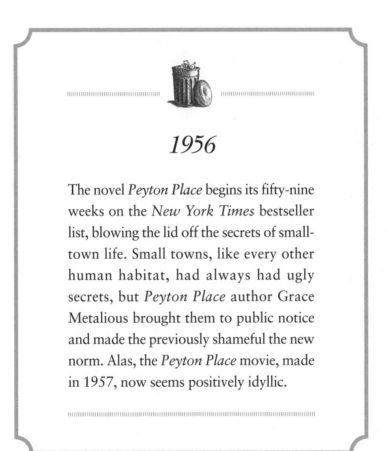

1956

The novel *Peyton Place* begins its fifty-nine weeks on the *New York Times* bestseller list, blowing the lid off the secrets of small-town life. Small towns, like every other human habitat, had always had ugly secrets, but *Peyton Place* author Grace Metalious brought them to public notice and made the previously shameful the new norm. Alas, the *Peyton Place* movie, made in 1957, now seems positively idyllic.

1962

Marilyn Monroe—who may or may not have had affairs with both John and Robert Kennedy—sings a breathy "Happy Birthday, Mr. President" to John F. Kennedy at Madison Square Garden. Her dress is so tight that she had to be sewn into it. At least Monroe doesn't jump out of the cake.

1965

Following surgery to remove his gall blad-
der, President Lyndon Baines Johnson lifts
his shirt, exposes a wide expanse of
paunch, and shows off the incision to the
White House press corps.

1968

The Hays Office closes. From 1930, Hollywood studios had voluntarily submitted to the benign censorship of the Hays Code, named after the Office's first director, Presbyterian elder Will Hays. The Code proscribed certain on-camera behaviors (such as ridiculing the clergy, sexual perversion, and drug trafficking) and compelled studios to require that movie stars sign morals clauses. Seen any good movies lately?

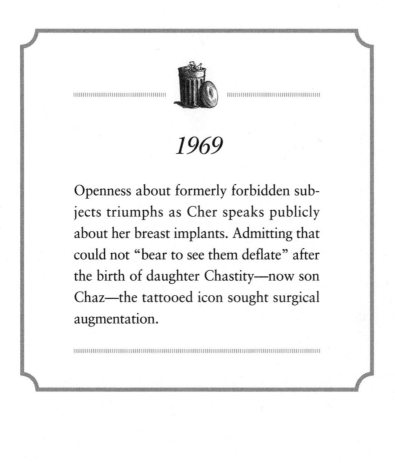

1969

Openness about formerly forbidden subjects triumphs as Cher speaks publicly about her breast implants. Admitting that could not "bear to see them deflate" after the birth of daughter Chastity—now son Chaz—the tattooed icon sought surgical augmentation.

1969

California governor Ronald Reagan signs the nation's first no-fault divorce law. It seemed so civilized at the time. The divorce rate was 9.2 percent in 1960; now it is around 50 percent. So much for the family as the civilizing unit of society.

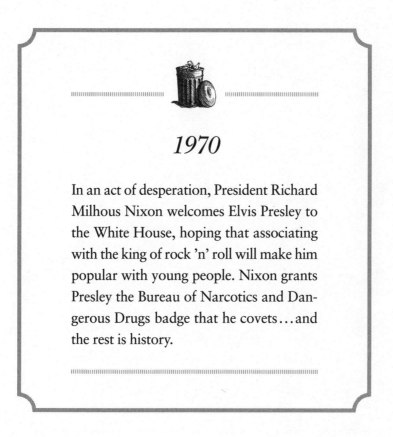

1970

In an act of desperation, President Richard Milhous Nixon welcomes Elvis Presley to the White House, hoping that associating with the king of rock 'n' roll will make him popular with young people. Nixon grants Presley the Bureau of Narcotics and Dangerous Drugs badge that he covets...and the rest is history.

1973

An American Family, featuring private moments with the Loud family of affluent Santa Barbara, debuts as TV's first reality show. On PBS! Ten million viewers watch son Lance come out of the closet as gay, and *TV Guide* names the moment when Pat Loud throws Bill, her husband of twenty-one years, out of the house as one of the "Top 100 Television Moments."

1973

Also in this pivotal year for White Trash Normal, the "Battle of the Sexes" match takes place between Wimbledon champions Billie Jean King and Bobby Riggs at the Houston Astrodome. Riggs arrives in a chariot pulled by women, while Ms. King makes her entrance in a litter held aloft by football players in togas. It's official: King and Riggs have turned the once aristocratic game of tennis into a plebeian farce. King hails the match as an advance for women's tennis.

1977

Billy Beer. In one of many less than Jeffersonian moments of President Jimmy [sic] Carter's tenure, the Falls City Brewing Company launches Billy Beer, named in honor of the president's embarrassing younger brother Billy, a precursor to the even more embarrassing Roger Clinton. Another WT milestone: little Amy is allowed to read a book at the table during a state dinner.

1982

Space alien E.T. in the eponymous movie is sort of cute, but the foul-mouthed moppets who befriend him (played by Drew Barrymore, Robert MacNaughton, and Henry Thomas) should have had their mouths washed out with soap.

1992

Vice President Dan Quayle criticizes *Murphy Brown* because the title character, a rich, powerful TV anchor, opts to become a single mother and won't even reveal the father. There is a powerful outcry in the media—against Dan Quayle.

1992

Creepy old stepdad Woody Allen, fifty-seven, goes public with his relationship with Soon-Yi, twenty, adopted daughter of Mia Farrow, the cultural icon's significant other. (The two married in 1997.) If only Mia hadn't stumbled upon Woody's stash of Soon-Yi nudie pics! But don't these supposed New York sophisticates belong in a swamp?

1994

Olympic figure skater Nancy Kerrigan is attacked and clubbed on the knee during a practice session, temporarily forcing Kerrigan out of competition. Rival Tonya Harding's ex-husband, Jeff Gillooly, goes to jail, insisting Tonya was in on it. Rather than being dismissed as too trashy for words, the story leads the evening news.

1994

Yes, it was a very good year for White Trash Normal, as TV host Jerry Springer, in a quest to beef up falling ratings, revamps his relatively staid talk show, introducing brawl-provoking paternity tests—often with interfamily findings— boyfriends who turn out to be girls, and randy grannies who sleep with sons-in-law. The fun starts when Jerry slides down a pole at the start of every show!

1995

A pioneer in letting it all hang out, Princess Diana spills the (intimate) beans on her royal marriage in an interview for *Panorama* with Martin Bashir. Of course, HRH Prince Charles had beaten her to the punch by giving journalist Jonathan Dimbleby an interview on the breakdown of his marriage the previous year. Why should the Loud family have all the fun?

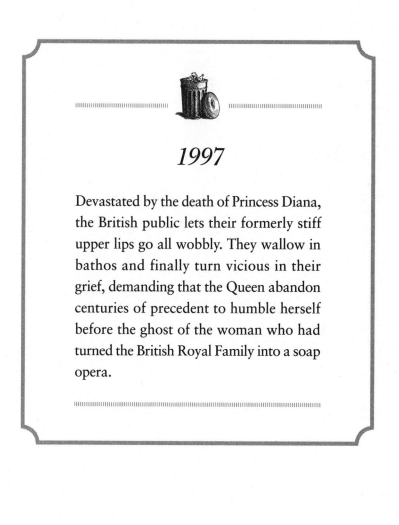

1997

Devastated by the death of Princess Diana, the British public lets their formerly stiff upper lips go all wobbly. They wallow in bathos and finally turn vicious in their grief, demanding that the Queen abandon centuries of precedent to humble herself before the ghost of the woman who had turned the British Royal Family into a soap opera.

1998

The president of the United States looks into the camera and declares, "I did not have sexual relations with that woman—Miss Lewinsky." Monica Lewinsky, nineteen at the time of the escapade, is ruined, but the public soon forgives the loveable imp in the Oval Office.

1998

Zara Phillips, seventeen, Queen Elizabeth II's granddaughter, shows up at the Prince of Wales's fiftieth birthday party sporting a tongue piercing. What more can one say?

1999

A cell phone rings repeatedly during a Broadway performance of *The Lion in Winter* and a furious Laurence Fishburne stops the show to curse the ring-ring boor. Fishburne uses the F-word, so maybe he doesn't fully deserve the resulting standing ovation. But we all know how he felt.

1999

In the same year that the cell phone scourge comes to a crisis, old family heirlooms become "bling bling" as we all learn to speak hip hop.

2003

Not Quite Sir Walter Raleigh, Rolling Stone Mick Jagger nevertheless becomes Sir Mick in a ceremony at Buckingham Palace. Sighs of relief when Sir Mick doesn't trash the place! Kudos: Queen Elizabeth II suddenly remembers she has a previous engagement and delegates the chore to the Prince of Wales.

2010

Snooki, the reality TV star whose special talents include getting drunk and throwing up on camera, makes Barbara Walters's "Ten Most Fascinating People" list. Was the Octomom not available?

2011

Whatever happened to Presbyterian punch and green mints? Kim Kardashian and Kris Humphries begin their seventy-two-day marriage with—what else?—reality TV nuptials. The sacred moment is aired on E! Kim's take for photos reportedly runs into the millions. Perhaps stating the obvious, Kris later calls the wedding "a sham." Don't worry about Kim. She and boyfriend Kanye West—no nups here!— are happy parents of new baby girl North West. Kris Jenner, Kim's thoughtful stepfather, reportedly acquires a $4 million deal for baby pics.

2012

Chivalry is officially declared dead as the *Costa Concordia* sinks off the coast of Tuscany and male passengers and crew members elbow past and knock down women and children to save their own sorry skins. Comparisons to sinking of the *Titanic*—when gentlemen, whether of first class or steerage, observed the "women and children first" rule—prove unflattering.

2012

White Trash milestones come thick and fast as *Here Comes Honey Boo Boo*, featuring a cornucopia of social ills, becomes the TLC network's top reality show. Honey Boo Boo's mom, June Shannon, has four daughters fathered by four different men. She can only remember the names of three dads. Honey Boo Boo's father, Sugar Bear Thompson—who, alas, has done prison time—is unforgettable.

2012

"Actress and humanitarian" Angelina Jolie—who is also the unwed mother of six children, three biological and three adopted—is named a UN Special Envoy for refugees. She did have the Billy Bob Thornton tattoos removed after hooking up with Brad Pitt. Still, she's not quite Daniel Patrick Moynihan.

2012

For those who thought Richard Nixon's buddy BeBe Rebozo, the oft-investigated Florida banker, was a bit much, meet presidential pal 2.0 Jay-Z, purveyor of such classics as "Bitches and Sisters." The prez and Jay-Z had so much fun flying around the country on Air Force One! Then the rapper had to go and ruin a beautiful friendship by implying that President Obama had been instrumental in helping the rapper and wife Beyoncé go to Cuba.

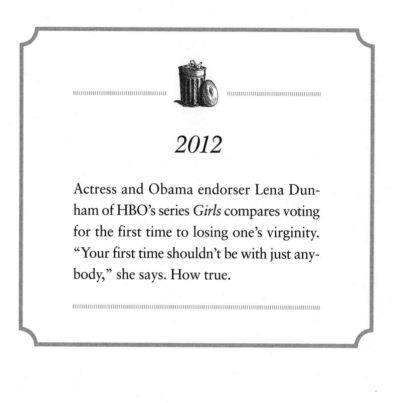

2012

Actress and Obama endorser Lena Dunham of HBO's series *Girls* compares voting for the first time to losing one's virginity. "Your first time shouldn't be with just anybody," she says. How true.

2012

Former sartorial advisor to Vice President Al Gore, feminist author Naomi Wolf turns Boswell and writes a biography of ... her vagina. *Vagina, a New Biography* was inspired by Ms. Wolf's reflections on the quality of her orgasms. Thanks for sharing.

2012

Winston Churchill, thou shouldst be living at this hour: UK Prime Minister and Old Etonian David Cameron goes on the *Letterman* show and can't quite translate the words Magna Carta into English. In fact, he can't quite place the Magna Carta. Which is worse? An Old Etonian who flubs the seminal document of English liberty? Or a prime minister who goes on *Letterman*?

2013

The White Trashing of America continues to accelerate as *Teen Mom* TV reality-show star Farrah Abraham, twenty-two, checks into rehab. Does this mean she won't keep making her sex tapes? In other news, Miss Abraham has recently traded her C-cups for D-cup breast implants.

2013

Whose side is she on, anyway? Episcopal Presiding Bishop Katharine Jefferts Schori shows that divinity school ain't what it used to be when she denounces St. Paul for driving out a slave girl's demons. The bishop regards this as "depriving her of her gift of spiritual awareness." And you thought dancing Eucharist was bad?

2013

Clueless actress Alicia Silverstone launches a breastfeeding milk bank for vegan mothers. Kind Mama Milk Share (are you feeling queasy yet?) was inspired by the plight of a Silverstone friend who had trouble breastfeeding after a surgical breast reduction. Apparently, she was surprised to find this impeded nursing. But at least she has some standards—she doesn't eat meat.

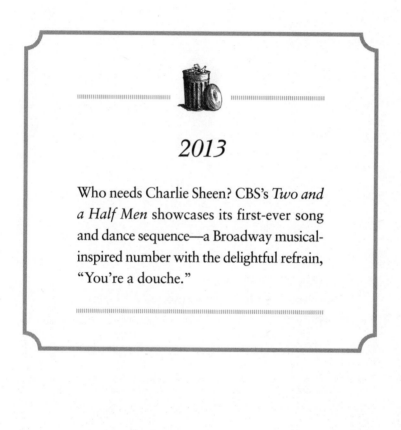

2013

Who needs Charlie Sheen? CBS's *Two and a Half Men* showcases its first-ever song and dance sequence—a Broadway musical-inspired number with the delightful refrain, "You're a douche."

2013

Got bondage? *Fifty Shades of Grey*, a mix of erotica and atrocious writing, becomes the bestselling book of all time in Britain, displacing *Harry Potter*. Married women largely account for the book's success, which is why it was dubbed "Mommy Porn."

Bibliography

"'16 and Pregnant' star arrested over stolen pregnancy test is not pregnant." Fox News, March 3, 2012. http://www.foxnews.com/entertainment/2012/03/03/16-and-pregnant-star-arrested-over-stolen-pregnancy-test-is-not-pregnant/.

Allison, Dorothy. *Bastard Out of Carolina*. New York: Dutton, 1992.

Alvarez, Manny. "Do's and Don'ts for Safe Body Piercing." Dr. Manny's Health Beat. Fox News, November 17, 2006. http://www.foxnews.com/story/0,2933,230101,00.html.

Bankhead, Charles. "More Debt Means More Obesity, Study Says." ABC News, August 9, 2009.

Bauerlein, Mark. "Pride and Indecency." *Chronicle of Higher Education*, September 19, 2012. http://chronicle.com/blogs/conversation/2012/09/19/pride-and-indecency/.

Berger, Steve. "Raised by White Trash." CreateSpace Independent Publishing Platform. 2011.

"Birds, Bees, and Bias: How Absent Sex Ed Standards Fail New York's Students." New York Civil Liberties Union. September 2012. http://www.nyclu.org/files/publications/NYCLU_SexEd_report.pdf.

Brooks, Arthur C. "My Valuable, Cheap College Degree." *New York Times*, January 31, 2013. http://www.nytimes.com/2013/02/01/opinion/my-valuable-cheap-college-degree.html.

Brown, Dan. *The Da Vinci Code*. New York: Doubleday, 2003.

Brown, Douglas. "Tattoo fans see reason to smile through painful bouts of rib ink." *Denver Post*, October 4, 2011. http://www.denverpost.com/lifestyles/ci_19034387.

Bunch, Sonny. "Service with a Snarl." *Washington Free Beacon*, February 6, 2013.

Clifford, Stephanie. "Would You Like a Smile with That?" *New York Times*, August 6, 2011. http://www.nytimes.com/2011/08/07/business/pret-a-manger-with-new-fast-food-ideas-gains-a-foothold-in-united-states.html?pagewanted=all.

Crossan, John Dominic. *The Historical Jesus: The Life of a Mediterranean Jewish Peasant*. New York: HarperOne, 1993.

Culp-Ressler, Tara. "STUDY: New York Public Schools Have 'Shocking' Gaps in Sex Education." Think Progress. September 14, 2012. http://thinkprogress.org/health/2012/09/14/849911/study-new-york-sex-education/.

Dalrymple, Theodore. "It Hurts, Therefore I Am." *City Journal 5*, no. 4 (Autumn 1995). http://www.city-journal. org/html/5_4_oh_to_be.html.

Day, Clarence. *Life with Father*. Mattituck, NY: Amereon, 1981.

DeMello, Margo. *Bodies of Inscription: A Cultural History of the Modern Tattoo Community*. Durham, NC: Duke University Press, 2000.

Douthat, Ross. *Bad Religion: How We Became a Nation of Heretics*. New York: Free Press, 2012.

"Do You Know How Food Portions Have Changed in the Past 20 Years?" National Heart, Lung, and Blood Institute Obesity Education Initiative, 2003.

Ensler, Eve. *The Vagina Monologues*. Dramatists Play Service, 2000.

Faulkner, William. *Snopes: A Triology*. New York: Modern Library, 2012.

Flurowaves. "I wish I had an extra finger then I could grab more cheeseballs." YouTube. October 26, 2012. http:// www.youtube.com/watch?v=IT2ibEkUBQA.

Franklin, Benjamin. *Poor Richard's Almanack*. New York: Barnes & Noble, 2004.

Frey, James. *The Final Testament of the Holy Bible*. New York: Gagosian Gallery, 2011.

Galván, Veronica V., Rosa S. Vessal, and Matthew T. Golley. "The Effects of Cell Phone Conversations on the Attention and Memory of Bystanders." *PLOS ONE*. March 13, 2013. http://www.plosone.org/article/ info%3Adoi%2F10.1371%2Fjournal.pone.0058579.

Gasparino, Charles. "A 'deadbeat' bailout: Team Bam's blow to housing." *New York Post*, February 10, 2012.

Gibbon, Edward. *The Decline and Fall of the Roman Empire*. Edited by Hans-Friedrich Mueller. Modern Library Classics. New York: Random House, 2003.

Gilbert, Elizabeth. *Eat, Pray, Love: One Woman's Search for Everything Across Italy, India, and Indonesia*. New York: Viking Penguin, 2006.

Gliatto, Tom. "Life After *The Swan*." *People* 62, no. 5 (August 2, 2004). http://www.people.com/people/archive/article/0,,20150694,00.html.

Grim, Ryan, Arthur Delaney, and Lucia Graves. "Learning to Walk: Fear, Shame and Your Underwater Mortgage." Huffington Post, February 3, 2011. http://www.huffingtonpost.com/2011/02/03/learning-to-walk-underwater-mortgages_n_818315.html.

Heath, Hadley. "Mr. President, Please Stop Subsidizing College." The Blaze, May 6, 2012. http://www.theblaze.com/contributions/mr-president-please-stop-subsidizing-college/.

"Here Comes Honey Boo Boo family is now 'taking home $20,000 an episode after TLC gave them a huge raise.'" *Daily Mail*, October 1, 2012. http://www.dailymail.co.uk/femail/article-2211228/Here-Comes-Honey-Boo-Boo-family-taking-home-20-000-episode-TLC-gave-huge-raise.html.

Holmes, Oliver Wendell. *The Autocrat of the Breakfast Table*. 2 vols. Boston and New York: Houghton, Mifflin, 1894.

Humphrys, John. "My study of manners." *Telegraph*, October 18, 2012. http://www.telegraph.co.uk/culture/books/booknews/9611647/John-Humphrys-My-study-of-manners.html.

"Incidence, Prevalence, and Cost of Sexually Transmitted Infections in the United States." CDC Fact Sheet,

February 2013. http://www.cdc.gov/std/stats/sti-estimates-fact-sheet-feb-2013.pdf.

James, E. L. *Fifty Shades Trilogy: Fifty Shades of Grey, Fifty Shades Darker, Fifty Shades Freed.* New York: Vintage, 2012.

Jameson, Marni. "As Americans' debt has soared, so has obesity." *Orlando Sentinel*, August 6, 2011. http://articles.orlandosentinel.com/2011-08-06/health/os-debt-obesity-20110806_1_debt-counseling-obesity-incharge-debt-solutions.

Jefferson, Thomas. *Notes on the State of Virginia.* Edited by William Peden. Chapel Hill: University of North Carolina Press for the Institute of Early American History and Culture, Williamsburg, Virginia, 1954. Available online as vol. 1, chapter 18, document 16 of *The Founder's Constitution*. University of Chicago Press. http://press-pubs.uchicago.edu/founders/documents/v1ch18s16.html.

Johnson, Rachel, Jenni Murray, Sue Perkins, and Alexander McCall Smith, introduced by Lynn Truss. "How to get by in our rude new world: Fed up with ill-mannered people? Then take a tip from our etiquette experts." *Telegraph*, October 13, 2012. http://www.telegraph.co.uk/lifestyle/9606388/How-to-get-by-in-our-rude-new-world.html.

Keith, Toby and Scotty Emerick. "Can't Buy You Money." *White Trash with Money*, 2006.

Klein, Herbert S. "The Changing American Family." *Hoover Digest*, no. 3 (2004). http://www.hoover.org/publications/hoover-digest/article/6798.

Krueger, David and John Mann. *The Secret Language of Money: How to Make Smarter Financial Decisions and Live a Richer Life.* New York: McGraw Hill, 2009.

Last, Jonathan V. *What to Expect When No One's Expecting: America's Coming Demographic Disaster.* New York: Encounter, 2013.

Lisitude, "First Time—Lena Dunham for Obama on Voting First Time." YouTube. October 25, 2012. http://www.youtube.com/watch?v=d3jzyKF6M7g.

Lowry, Rich. "'Dude, Where's My Lifeboat?'" National Review Online, January 17, 2012. http://www.nationalreview.com/articles/288253/dude-where-s-my-lifeboat-rich-lowry.

———. "Heed the 99 Percent: They Have a Point, but Not the One They Think." National Review Online, October 14, 2011. http://www.nationalreview.com/articles/280104/heed-99-percent-rich-lowry.

Lusardi, Annamaria, Daniel Schneider, and Peter Tufano. "Financially Fragile Households: Evidence and Implications." *Brookings Papers on Economic Activity.* Spring 2011. http://www.brookings.edu/~/media/projects/bpea/spring%202011/2011a_bpea_lusardi.pdf.

Mains, Geoff. *Urban Aboriginals: A Celebration of Leathersexuality.* 3rd ed. Los Angeles: Daedalus, 2002.

McCarthy, Ellen. "On Love: We Couldn't Have Scripted It Any Better." *Washington Post*, February 14, 2013. http://articles.washingtonpost.com/2013-02-14/lifestyle/37094259_1_alexander-photography-classes-happy-holiday.

Messina, Lynn. "I Don't Want My Preschooler to Be a 'Gentleman.'" *New York Times*, January 10, 2013. http://parenting.blogs.nytimes.com/2013/01/10/i-dont-want-my-preschooler-to-be-a-gentleman/?_r=0.

Meyer, Dick. *Why We Hate Us: American Discontent in the New Millenium.* New York: Broadway, 2009.

Murray, Charles. *Coming Apart: The State of White America, 1960–2010.* New York: Crown Forum, 2012.

Noah, Tim. "Labor of Love: The enforced happiness of Pret A Manger." *New Republic*, February 1, 2013. http://www.newrepublic.com/article/112204/pret-manger-when-corporations-enforce-happiness#.

Nocera, Joe. "In Prison for Taking a Liar Loan." *New York Times*, March 25, 2011. http://www.nytimes.com/2011/03/26/business/26nocera.html?pagewanted=all&_r=0.

PaulWinterConsort. "Winter Solstice Celebration at New York's Cathedral of St. John the Divine." YouTube. June 9, 2010. http://www.youtube.com/watch?v=N64tBKDqM_o.

Percy, Walker. *Lost in the Cosmos: The Last Self-Help Book.* New York: Farrar, Straus and Giroux, 1983.

Pew Research Center. "Tattooed Gen Nexters." December 9, 2008. http://www.pewresearch.org/daily-number/tattooed-gen-nexters/.

Povoledo, Elisabetta. "Pope Calls for 'Peace in all the World' in First Easter Message." *New York Times*, March 31, 2013. http://www.nytimes.com/2013/04/01/world/europe/pope-francis-calls-for-peace-in-all-the-world-in-first-easter-message.html?_r=5&.

Rashad, Inas, Michael Grossman, and Shin-Li Chou, "The Super Size of America: An Economic Estimation of Body Mass Index and Obesity in Adults." National Bureau of Economic Research Working Paper Series 11584. August 2005. http://www.nber.org/papers/w11584.pdf?new_window=1.

Ratzinger, Joseph (Pope Benedict XVI). *Jesus of Nazareth: The Infancy Narratives.* New York: Image, 2012.

Riley, Naomi Schaeffer. "Porn by Equinox: And Your Kids Can't Miss It." *New York Post*, March 17, 2013. http://www.nypost.com/p/news/opinion/opedcolumnists/porn_by_equinox_XIHR4gfEtwuT128EPcfqZP.

Ritchel, Matt. "Eat, Drink, Be Nice." *New York Times*, December 26, 2012. http://www.nytimes.com/2012/12/27/garden/eat-drink-be-nice-teaching-children-manners.html?pagewanted=all.

Rob (commenter). Comment on the 2002 Winter Solstice Celebration at the Cathedral of John the Divine. "Solstice Recollections." http://solsticeconcert.com/recollections/?p=1.

Rohrer, Finlo. "So why do 'normal' people get tattoos?" BBC News Magazine, October 9, 2007. http://news.bbc.co.uk/2/hi/7034500.stm.

Singletary, Michelle. "Seeking loan modifications shouldn't make homeowners target of scorn." *Washington Post*, October 20, 2010. http://www.washingtonpost.com/wp-dyn/content/article/2010/10/20/AR2010102006160.html.

Skenazy, Lenore, "'Lean In' and the Era of the Inconvenienced Mom." *Wall Street Journal*, March 24, 2013. http://online.wsj.com/article/SB1000142412788732341530457837101157867105 2.html?mod=googlenews_wsj.

Smith, Emily Esfahani. "For Camille Paglia, the Spiritual Quest Defines All Great Art." Daily Beast, December 17, 2012. http://www.thedailybeast.com/newsweek/2012/12/16/for-camille-paglia-the-spiritual-quest-defines-all-great-art.html.

Street, Chriss. "College Graduates Are the New Debt Slaves." Testosterone Pit. February 5, 2013.

Talbot, Margaret. "Little Hotties." *New Yorker*, December 4, 2006.

Toynbee, Arnold. *A Study of History*. 12 vols. Oxford: Oxford University Press, 1934–61.

Travis, Merle. "Sixteen Tons." Recorded by Tennessee Ernie Ford in 1955.

Truss, Lynne. *How Rude!: Modern Manners Defined*. Waitrose, 2012.

Twenge, Jean. *Generation Me: Why Today's Young Americans Are More Confident, Assertive, Entitled—and More Miserable Than Ever*. New York: Free Press, 2006.

Walls, Jeannette. *The Glass Castle: A Memoir*. New York: Scriber, 2006.

Waugh, Evelyn. *Brideshead Revisited*. New York: Back Bay, 2012.

Whitley, David. "Colin Kaepernick ushers in an inked-up NFL quarterbacking era." *Sporting News*, November 28, 2012. http://www.sportingnews.com/nfl/story/2012-11-28/colin-kaepernick-tattoos-49ers-qb-start-alex-smith-stats-contract-draft.

Whyte, David. *The Heart Aroused: Poetry and the Preservation of Soul in Corporate America*. New York: Random House, 2002.

———. *Pilgrim: Poems*. Langley, WA: Many Rivers, 2012.

Wiles, Russ. "Lack of financial savvy hinders youth in debt." *Arizona Republic*, April 25, 2011. http://www.azcentral.com/arizonarepublic/business/articles/20110424arizona-middle-class-young-adults-lack-financial-savvy.html.

Wilson, A. N. "Whatever happened to women and children first?" *Daily Mail*, January 17, 2012. http://www.dailymail.co.uk/debate/article-2087585/Cruise-ship-Costa-Concordia-sinking-Whatever-happened-women-children-first.html.

Yousuf, Hibba. "Nicholas Cage: Movie star, foreclosure victim: Hollywood actor's financial troubles continue as he loses two New Orleans homes worth $6.8 million in foreclosure action." CNN Money, November 16, 2009. http://money.cnn.com/2009/11/13/real_estate/Nicolas_Cage/.

Index

F-word, the, 11, 138, 166

G
Galt, John, 17
Gara, Kristy, 16
Gasparino, Charles, 40
Gatorade®, 23
Gaul, 126
"Generation Broke," 40
Generation Me: Why Today's Young Americans Are More Confident, Assertive, Entitled—and More Miserable than Ever Before, 79
Generation Nexters (Gen Nexters), 2–3
Genesis, 78
Georgetown, 70
Giant, 136
Gibbon, Edward, 12
Gillooly, Jeff, 160
"Ginny," 128, 131
Glass Castle, The, 31
God, 35, 57, 70–73, 78, 135
Goldilocks, 120
Goldsmith's department store, 57
Good Friday, 70
Good Wife, The, 94
Gore, Al, 176
Great Aunt Fannie, 31
Greenville, MI, 71
Gregg, Bentley, 95
Grey's Anatomy, 96
Gunlock, Julie, 61
Gypsy, 57

H